The Organizational Basis of Leisure Participation

A Motivational Exploration

Robert A. Stebbins

University of Calgary

The Organizational Basis of Leisure Participation

A Motivational Exploration

Robert A. Stebbins
University of Calgary

 Venture Publishing, Inc. • *State College, PA*

Production Manager: Richard Yocum
Manuscript Editing: Michele L. Barbin
Cover Design: Echelon Design
Cover Photo from the Glenbow Archives NA-5327-706

Library of Congress Catalogue Card Number 2002109286
ISBN 1-892132-38-9

Table of Contents

Chapter Four
Volunteer and Leisure Service Organizations ... 47

Chapter Five
Tribes 63

Chapter Six
Social Worlds 73

Chapter Seven
Social Movements 87

Chapter Eight
Implications 101

Acknowledgments

I wish to express my gratitude to Michele Barbin, copyeditor of this book, for a superb job of editing and expeditious shepherding of the manuscript through the critical stage of its production.

Introduction

The question of why people choose to participate in certain leisure activities rather than others has fascinated no small number of philosophers and social scientists, starting with Aristotle and continuing to present-day specialists in leisure studies. This enormously complicated issue still moves modern thinkers to ponder it. Although a motivational question—about that there is no doubt—treating it as a purely psychological matter results in too narrow an explanation. Leisure participation is also motivated by a variety of social conditions—many of them organizational in character. Here, as in most areas of life, action is structured or organized in interpersonal relationships, small groups, social networks, and grassroots associations as well as in larger, more complex organizations, and still more broadly, in social worlds and social movements. Each type of organization shapes, in its own distinctive way, the values, actions, and attitudes of its members.

This book shows that studying the social organization in this sphere of social life can be wonderfully fruitful, and lead to numerous insights about why people participate in leisure, in general, and certain leisure activities, in particular. Social organization is used here as shorthand for the range of collectivities that add social and psychological structure to leisure life, extending from dyads, small groups, and social networks through larger organizations, notably tribes, social worlds, and social movements. Consequently, discussion in this book centers on these different types of leisure organizations rather than on a community or societal organization of leisure. Following extensive discussion in Chapters 2 through 7 about how leisure participation is substantially shaped by the organizational form being considered, the final chapter traces some implications of this relationship for research and practice in leisure studies.

The subfield of leisure organizations, if it in fact amounts to a subfield, is not exactly brimming with theoretical frameworks and empirical research although there are some exceptions to this observation on the research side. Small leisure groups, most prominent among them family and adolescent formations, have been reasonably well-studied. The same may be said for some of the larger leisure organizations. However, other types of leisure collectivities are, for the most part, neglected. Theoretical and empirical material on these latter types is widely scattered and, as often as not, approached from a perspective quite different from the one developed here.

Thus, a further contribution of this book is that it pulls together relevant theory and research into a common framework. This framework consists of the concept of social organization, the multitude of reasons why it is important for understanding leisure participation, the way free time is organized as serious and casual leisure, and the way these relate to everyday and optimal leisure lifestyles. This framework is presented in Chapter 1.

Chapter One

The Importance of Social Organization

Social organization is one of those grand social science concepts that is most widely discussed and examined in the fields of sociology, anthropology, and management, and in one way or another makes its appearance in nearly every empirical and theoretical analysis of social life. Always there, though more often in the wings than at center stage, social organization seems constantly in danger of being taken for granted, or somewhat less seriously thus being given short shrift. Leisure studies, among the many social sciences, is not really being singled out in this sweeping condemnation. Rather this book examines leisure studies as a sort of demonstration project, since much can be learned about why people participate in leisure in general, and certain leisure activities, in particular, by studying the social organization of this sphere of life.

What is *social organization*? Guy Rocher defines it as

> the total arrangement of all the elements which serve to structure social action into a whole, which has an image or a particular form which is different from its constituent parts and also different from other possible arrangements. (1972, p. 149)

In leisure, as in many other areas of life, action is structured or organized in small groups, social networks, and grassroots organizations as well as in larger complex organizations, and still more broadly, in tribes (Maffesoli, 1996), social worlds, and social movements. Each structures the social behavior of its members in particular ways; some being unique to that kind of organization.

Still, Rocher's definition fails to consider a central aspect of organizational life: individual interests also structure organizations of every sort by instituting structures in the first place. Thus participating in leisure organizations, as with other kinds, amounts to a two-way street of influence from individual to collectivity and collectivity to individual. This is the first of three critical assumptions on which this book is based.

The second critical assumption is that members of these different types of organizations (defined in the widest sense of the word) know they are members. Third, these people highly value their membership. Granted we are considering only leisure organizations entered without coercion since members would abandon them if they were disvalued. When organizations are highly valued, belonging becomes an important motive for engaging in one or more of the leisure activities the organization promotes and facilitates.

The Meaning of Leisure Organizations

Consistent with usage in the preceding paragraph, the term *organization* will be used throughout this book to refer to all collective entities, running from the two-person dyad to the most global types—the tribe, the social world, and the social movement. Leisure organizations appear to hold a variety of meanings for their members. First, any organization is important to its members, because through it, they find a sense of belonging to a *distinctive* and *identifiable* part of the larger human world in which they live. Be that organization a friendship, poker club, political party, or international network of ham radio operators, each member feels the distinctiveness that comes from being included in it while nonmembers are excluded from it. Moreover, the organization in question can be identified and described; it has a *social reality* of its own for both members and outsiders who are aware of it (Borgatta, 1981). People know what is meant when John says he is a friend of Mary, and Joe says he plays poker every Friday night with a small group of regulars. Likewise, they understand when Pat says she belongs to such-and-such political party, and Sarah, a ham radio operator, says she is in contact with like-minded enthusiasts the world over.

It is a short step from the senses of distinctiveness and social reality of the organization to acquiring both *a social and a personal identity* related to it. A member's identity is social when other people (both members and nonmembers) recognize that person as member, as Mary's friend, as participant in the Friday night poker bash, and so on. This identity becomes personal when members present themselves to others as belonging to this-or-that political party, or as using a ham radio to enjoy some international conversation. Thus, by belonging to organizations, people carve out special places for themselves in the vast sea of humankind both socially and personally. In this way we begin to distinguish ourselves from the rest. Of course, leisure is not the only area of life where this happens, since many people also belong to work and family organizations. Some people are trapped in identifiable social arrangements, among them prisoners, battered wives, and people whose disease or disability makes them highly dependent on particular services or individuals. Still, leisure appears to offer the widest range of possibilities for organizational membership, and since leisure is chosen for the most part, it offers the widest range of attractive memberships.

The list of ways members define their organizations does not end here. For instance, all organizations offer some sort of *power and control* to their members. Two or three people can often do more than one person or perhaps do it better (e.g., lift an object, accomplish a task), and they may, as a dyad or triad, be more persuasive, more daring, even more intelligent than one person alone. Many a complex organization has the capacity to get what it wants, although usually only some of the time, as is evident with environmentalist pressure groups, amateur arts organizations, and collectivities that organize such diverse hobbyists as hunters, curling players, and barbershop singers. The considerable influence on American politics of the National Rifle Association, although exceptional for a leisure organization, illustrates this proposition about power and control well. Of course, no organization, however large or small, always gets exactly what it wants, nor do individual members always get the organization to do their bidding. So for all concerned, power and control are inevitably limited to some extent, even if these elements are omnipresent and give special meaning to organizational membership. The play of these two processes gives substance to the first critical assumption mentioned earlier.

Moving to a different plane, organizations can also be seen to help structure everyday living. That is, they do more than organize relations among people; they also organize some of their *time* according to a daily, weekly, monthly, or yearly schedule—or a combination of these. Close friendships impose daily or nearly daily commitments of time spent together for talking, doing something, or just being in one another's presence. Many sports and performing arts groups hold daily or weekly practice sessions. The aforementioned poker players assemble each week. The volunteer executives of a community organization often meet monthly, while the organization as a whole schedules one annual meeting for all members.

In addition to temporal structuring, organizations also help determine some of the *spatial movements* of their members. To meet with each other, whether as friends, teammates or colleagues, requires that most members leave home or work to go to another part of the community or, in some instances, another part of the region, nation, even the planet. Leisure organizations often help their members become familiar with buildings and geographic points seldom if ever encountered during everyday domestic and occupational routines. Furthermore, the routes by which members reach these meeting places make up another facet of the spatial structuring that accompanies affiliation with an organization. Because people participate in leisure organizations, they must, to meet with other participants, pass through neighborhoods, deal with traffic patterns, observe land-use arrangements, and embark on travel they would not likely have encountered otherwise.

Considered together these six meanings of organizations—distinctiveness, social reality, personal and social identity, power and control, temporal structuring, and spatial structuring—serve as basis for a seventh meaning, although only for people who are unemployed, underemployed, or retired. For many of these people, leisure organizations resemble those in which they once worked in various ways. To the extent the unemployed, underemployed, or retired miss this organizational feature of everyday life, they can find it anew in their pursuit of collective free-time activities. Even for those gainfully employed in an organization to the extent they desire (e.g., full-time, part-time), they can find, should they crave more, *complementary organization* in the sphere of leisure. By the way, work organizations are not always of the large-scale variety. Like some leisure organizations, they can also be dyadic and triadic. Family grocery stores, two-person law firms, and small consulting agencies offer a few examples.

Do these meanings really help explain why people take part in leisure organizations, including ones referred to here as friendships? They seem to, although research that would supply data on these organizations, and others not yet identified, is only now getting underway (Stebbins, 2001a). Note, too, that some of these meanings may only develop once a person has joined an organization and participated in it for awhile (e.g., time, spatial movement). Whether an incentive for joining a leisure organization or an incentive for remaining in one, these seven meanings would seem to constitute a powerful force to lead people to establish such organizations, or if already established, to get involved with one or continue their membership in one. More broadly, the very fact that leisure organizations exist, and exist in great numbers, contributes significantly to the scientific explanation of why people join collective leisure activities.

Serious Leisure

The organizational side of a person's leisure lifestyle varies with the kind of leisure pursued. Indeed, it appears that every leisure activity presents a unique organizational pattern. Such a pattern in, for instance, the morning coffee klatch differs enormously from the one in amateur tennis. The first is typically limited in scope, constituted mainly of a small number of people who participate in it and the coffee shop or other space in which it routinely takes place. The second is vast, consisting of not only officials, instructors, and small groups of regular players, but also of tournaments, formal clubs, suppliers and repairers of equipment as well as the small public who watch the matches.

There is neither space for nor need to cover the organizational pattern of each major leisure activity here. Instead, these activities are grouped and discussed under the headings of serious leisure and casual leisure— two broad categories of leisure that will be shown in subsequent chapters to vary, sometimes extensively, along the lines of organizational structure.

Serious leisure is the systematic pursuit of an amateur, hobbyist, or volunteer activity sufficiently substantial and interesting in nature for the participant to find a career there acquiring and expressing a combination of its special skills, knowledge, and experience (Stebbins, 1992, p. 3). It is typically contrasted with *casual* or unserious leisure, which is considerably less substantial and offers no career of the sort just described. Although casual leisure is sometimes defined residually as all leisure falling outside the three main types of serious leisure, casual leisure is also defined as an immediately, intrinsically rewarding, relatively short-lived pleasurable activity requiring little or no special training to enjoy it (Stebbins, 1997a, p. 18).

Serious leisure is constituted of three types: amateurism, hobbyist activities, and career volunteering. Amateurs are found in art, science, sport, and entertainment, where they are inevitably linked in one way or another with professional counterparts who coalesce, along with the public whom the two groups share, into a three-way system of relations and relationships known as the P-A-P system. See the Appendix (p. 129) for further explanation of this system. Professionals are identified and defined according to theory developed in the social scientific study of the professions—a substantially more exact procedure than the ones relying on the simplistic and not infrequently commercially-shaped commonsense images of these workers. In other words, when studying amateurs and professionals descriptive definitions turn out to be too superficial, such as observing that the activity in question constitutes a livelihood for the second but not the first, or that the second works full-time at it whereas the first pursues it part-time. Rather, much more can be learned by noting that, the two are locked in, and therefore defined in most instances, by the P-A-P system.

Hobbyists lack the professional alter ego of amateurs, although they sometimes have commercial equivalents and often have small publics who take an interest in what they do. Hobbyists are classified according to five categories: collectors, makers and tinkerers, activity participants (in non-competitive, rule-based, pursuits such as backpacking and barbershop singing), players of sports and games (in competitive, rule-based activities with no professional counterparts such as long-distance running and competitive swimming), and enthusiasts of the liberal arts hobbies. The rules guiding rule-based pursuits are, for the most part, either subcultural (informal) or regulatory (formal). Thus seasoned hikers in the Rocky Mountains know they should, for example, stay on established trails, pack out all garbage, be prepared for changes in weather, and make noise to scare off bears. The liberal arts hobbyists are enamored of the systematic acquisition of knowledge for its own sake. Many of them accomplish this by reading voraciously in a field of art, sport, cuisine, language, culture, history, science, philosophy, politics, or literature (Stebbins, 1994). However, some of them go beyond this to expand their knowledge still further through cultural travel.

Volunteering is

> helping action of an individual…valued by him or her, and yet not aimed directly at material gain or mandated or coerced by others. Thus, in the broadest sense, *volunteering* is an uncoerced helping activity…engaged in not primarily for financial gain and not by coercion or mandate. It is thereby different…from work, slavery, or conscription. (Van Til, 1988, p. 5)

Such activity is oriented toward helping oneself or others or both. However, the field of serious leisure, or career volunteering, is narrower, even if it does cover considerable ground. The taxonomy published by Stebbins (1998a, pp. 74–80), which consists of sixteen types of organizational volunteering, shows the scope of career volunteering. Career volunteers provide a great variety of services in education, science, civic affairs (e.g., advocacy projects, professional and labor organizations), spiritual development, health, economic development, religion, politics, government (both programs and services), human relationships, recreation, and the arts. Some of these volunteers work in the fields of safety or the physical environment, while others prefer to provide necessities (e.g., food, clothing, shelter) or support services. Although much career volunteering appears to be connected in some way with an organization of some sort, the scope of this leisure is possibly even broader, perhaps including the kinds of help devoted individuals perform for social movements or for neighbors and family. Still, the definition of serious leisure restricts attention to volunteering in which the participant can find a career where there is more or less continuous and substantial helping. Therefore, one-time donations of money, blood, services, and the like are more accurately classified as voluntary action of another sort, as are instances of casual volunteering, which includes ushering, stuffing envelopes, and handing out programs as an aide for commercial, professional, or serious leisure undertakings (Stebbins, 1996c).

Serious leisure is defined by six distinguishing qualities (Stebbins, 1992, pp. 6–8) found among amateurs, hobbyists, and volunteers alike. One is the occasional need to *persevere*, such as in confronting danger (Fine, 1988, p. 181) or managing stage fright (Stebbins, 1981) or embarrassment (Floro, 1978, p. 198). Yet, it is clear that positive feelings about the activity come, to some extent, from sticking with it "through thick and thin," and conquering adversity. A second quality is, as already indicated, that of finding a *career* in the endeavor, shaped as it is by its own special contingencies, turning points, and stages of achievement or involvement. Because of the widespread tendency to see the idea of career as applying only to occupations, note that, in this definition, the term is much more broadly used, following Goffman's (1961, pp. 127–128) elaboration of the concept of "moral career." Broadly conceived of, careers are available in all substantial, complicated roles, including especially those in work, leisure, deviance, politics, religion, and interpersonal relationships.

Careers in serious leisure commonly rest on a third quality: significant personal *effort* based on specially acquired *knowledge, training*, or *skill,* and, indeed, all three at times. Examples include such characteristics as showmanship, athletic prowess, scientific knowledge, and long experience in a role. Fourth, eight *durable benefits*, or broad outcomes, of serious leisure have so far been identified, mostly from research on amateurs. They are self-actualization, self-enrichment, self-expression, regeneration or renewal of self, feelings of accomplishment, enhancement of self-image, social interaction and belongingness, and lasting physical products of the activity (e.g., a painting, scientific paper, piece of furniture). A ninth benefit—self-gratification, or the combination of superficial enjoyment and deep satisfaction—is also one of the main benefits of casual leisure if the enjoyment part dominates.

A fifth quality of serious leisure is the *unique ethos* that grows up around each instance of it, a central component of which is a special social world where participants can pursue their free-time interests. Unruh developed the following definition:

> A *social world* must be seen as a unit of social organization which is diffuse and amorphous in character. Generally larger than groups or organizations, social worlds are not necessarily defined by formal boundaries, membership lists, or spatial territory....A social world must be seen as an internally recognizable constellation of actors, organizations, events, and practices which have coalesced into a perceived sphere of interest and involvement for participants. Characteristically, a social world lacks a powerful centralized authority structure and is delimited by...effective communication and not territory nor formal group membership. (1980, p. 277)

In another paper Unruh added that the typical social world is characterized by voluntary identification, and by a freedom to enter into and depart from it (Unruh, 1979). Moreover, because it is so diffuse, ordinary members are only partly involved in the full range of its activities. After all, a social world may be local, regional, multiregional, national, even international. Third, people in complex societies such as Canada and the United States are often members of several social worlds. Finally, social worlds are held together, to an important degree, by semiformal or mediated communication. Social worlds are rarely heavily bureaucratized yet, due to their diffuseness, they are rarely characterized by intense face-to-face interaction. Rather, communication is typically mediated by newsletters, posted notices, telephone messages, mass mailings, Internet communications, radio and television announcements, and similar means, with the strong possibility that the Internet could become the most popular of these in the future.

The sixth quality revolves around the preceding five: participants in serious leisure tend to *identify* strongly with their chosen pursuits. In contrast, casual leisure, although hardly humiliating or despicable, is nonetheless too fleeting, mundane, and commonplace for most people to find a distinctive identity there.

In addition, research on serious leisure has led to the discovery of a distinctive set of rewards for each activity examined (Stebbins, 2001a, p. 13). In these studies the participant's leisure satisfaction has been found to stem from a constellation of particular rewards gained from the activity, be it boxing, ice climbing, or giving dance lessons to the elderly. Furthermore, the rewards are not only satisfying in themselves, but also satisfying as counterweights to the costs encountered in the activity. That is, every serious leisure activity contains its own combination of tensions, dislikes and disappointments that each participant must confront in some way. For instance, an amateur football player may not always like attending daily practices, being bested occasionally by more junior players when there, and being required to sit on the sidelines from time to time while others get experience at his position. Yet he may still regard this activity as highly satisfying—as serious leisure—because it also offers certain powerful rewards.

Put more precisely, the drive to find satisfaction in serious leisure is the drive to experience the rewards of a given leisure activity, such that its costs are seen by the participant as less significant by comparison. This is at once the meaning of the activity for the participant, and his or her motivation for engaging in it. This motivational sense of the concept of reward distinguishes it from the idea of durable benefit set out earlier—an idea that emphasizes outcomes rather than antecedent conditions. Nonetheless, the two ideas constitute two sides of the same social psychological coin.

The rewards of a serious leisure pursuit are the routine values that attract and hold its enthusiasts. Every serious leisure career both frames and is framed by the continuous search for these rewards—a search that takes months, and in many sports, years before the participant consistently finds deep satisfaction in his or her amateur, hobbyist, or volunteer role. The following ten rewards emerged in the course of various exploratory studies of amateurs, hobbyists, and career volunteers (for summary of these studies, see Stebbins, 2001a). As this list shows, the rewards of serious leisure are predominantly personal.

Personal Rewards

1. Personal enrichment (e.g., cherished experiences)

2. Self-actualization (e.g., developing skills, abilities, knowledge)

3. Self-expression (e.g., expressing skills, abilities, knowledge already developed)

4. Self-image (e.g., known to others as a particular kind of serious leisure participant)

5. Self-gratification (i.e., combination of superficial enjoyment and deep satisfaction)

6. Re-creation (i.e., regeneration) of oneself through serious leisure after a day's work

7. Financial return (i.e., from a serious leisure activity)

Social Rewards

8. Social attraction (e.g., associating with other serious leisure participants, associating with clients as a volunteer, participating in the social world of the activity)

9. Group accomplishment (e.g., group effort in accomplishing a serious leisure project; senses of helping, being needed, being altruistic)

10. Contribution to the maintenance and development of the group (e.g., senses of helping, being needed, being altruistic in making the contribution)

In the various studies on amateurs, hobbyists, and volunteers, these rewards, depending on the activity, were often given different weight by the interviewees to reflect their importance relative to each other. Nonetheless, some common ground exists. The studies on sport, for example, do show that, in terms of their personal importance, most serious leisure participants rank self-enrichment and self-gratification as number one and number two. Moreover, to find either reward, participants must have acquired sufficient levels of relevant skill, knowledge, and experience (Stebbins, 1979, 1993a). In other words, self-actualization, which was often ranked third in importance, is also highly rewarding in serious leisure.

Finally, amateurs, and sometimes even the activities they pursue, are marginal in society, for amateurs are neither dabblers nor professionals (see Stebbins, 1979). Moreover, the studies of hobbyists and career volunteers show that they, and some of their activities, are just as marginal and for many of the same reasons (Stebbins, 1996a, 1998b). Several properties of serious leisure give substance to these observations. One, although seemingly illogical, is that serious leisure is characterized empirically by an important degree of positive commitment to a pursuit (Stebbins, 1992, pp. 51–52). This commitment is measured, among other ways, by the sizeable investment of time and energy in the leisure made by its devotees and participants (considered further in Chapter 3). Two, serious leisure is pursued with noticeable intentness, with such passion that Erving Goffman (1963, pp. 144–145) once qualified amateurs and hobbyists as the "quietly disaffiliated." People with such orientations toward their leisure are marginal compared with people who go in for the ever popular forms of casual leisure.

Casual Leisure

Casual leisure has been defined as an immediately, intrinsically rewarding, relatively short-lived pleasurable activity requiring little or no special training to enjoy it (Stebbins, 1997a). Among its types are play (including dabbling), relaxation (e.g., sitting, napping, strolling), passive entertainment (e.g., television, books, recorded music), active entertainment (e.g., games of chance, party games), sociable conversation, sensory stimulation (e.g., sex, eating, drinking, sightseeing), and casual volunteering (described earlier). It is considerably less substantial and offers no career of the sort described for its counterpart, serious leisure (Stebbins, 1992). Casual leisure can also be defined residually as all leisure not classifiable as amateur, hobbyist, or career volunteering.

This brief review of the types of casual leisure reveals that they share at least one central property—all are hedonic. More precisely, all produce a significant level of pure pleasure or enjoyment for those participating in them. In broad, colloquial language, casual leisure could serve as the scientific term for the practice of doing what comes naturally. Yet, paradoxically, this leisure is by no means wholly frivolous, for there are some clear benefits in pursuing it. Moreover, unlike the evanescent hedonic property of casual leisure itself, its benefits are enduring—a property that makes them worthy of extended analysis in their own right.

Benefits

So far five benefits, or outcomes, of casual leisure have been identified. This is a preliminary list, so it is certainly possible that future research and theorizing could add to it (Stebbins, 2001c).

One lasting benefit of casual leisure is the *creativity and discovery* it sometimes engenders. Serendipity, "the quintessential form of informal experimentation, accidental discovery, and spontaneous invention" (Stebbins, 2001b), usually underlies these two processes. This suggests that serendipity and casual leisure are at times closely aligned. In casual leisure, as elsewhere, serendipity can lead to highly varied results, including a new understanding of a home gadget or government policy, a realization that a particular plant or bird exists in the neighborhood, or a different way of making artistic sounds on a musical instrument. Such creativity or discovery is unintended, however, and is therefore accidental. Moreover, it is not ordinarily the result of a problem-solving orientation of people taking part in casual leisure, since most of the time, they have little interest in trying to solve problems while engaging in such activity. Usually problems for which solutions must be found emerge at work or at home or during serious leisure. Another benefit springs from what has recently come to be known as *edutainment*. Nahrstedt (2000) holds that this benefit of casual leisure comes with participating in such mass entertainment as watching films and television programs, listening to popular music, and reading popular books and articles. Theme parks and museums are also considered sources of edutainment. While consuming media or frequenting places of this sort, these participants inadvertently learn something of substance about the social and physical world in which they live. They are, in a word, entertained and educated in the same breath.

Third, casual leisure affords *regeneration*, or re-creation, possibly even more so than its counterpart, serious leisure, since the latter can sometimes be intense. Of course, many a leisure studies specialist has observed that leisure in general affords relaxation or entertainment, if not both, and that these constitute two of its principal benefits. What is new in this observation is that it distinguishes between casual and serious leisure, and more importantly, it emphasizes the enduring effects of relaxation and entertainment when they help enhance overall equanimity, most notably in the interstices between periods of intense activity. Still, strange as it may seem, this blanket recognition of the importance of relaxation has not, according to Kleiber (2000), led to significant concern with regeneration in research and practice in leisure studies.

A fourth benefit that can flow from participation in casual leisure originates in the development and maintenance of *interpersonal relationships*. One of its types, the sociable conversation, is particularly fecund in this regard, but other types, when shared, as sometimes happens during sensory stimulation and passive and active entertainment, can also have the same effect. The interpersonal relationships in question are many and varied, and encompass those that form between friends, spouses, and members of families.

Well-being is another benefit that can flow from engaging in casual leisure. Speaking only for the realm of leisure, the greatest sense of well-being is achieved when a person develops an *optimal leisure lifestyle*. Such a lifestyle is "the deeply satisfying pursuit during free time of one or more substantial, absorbing forms of serious leisure, complemented by a judicious amount of casual leisure" (Stebbins, 2000a). People find optimal leisure lifestyles by partaking of leisure activities that individually and in combination realize human potential and enhance quality of life and well-being.

Organizations and Leisure Lifestyle

Lifestyle is

a distinctive set of shared patterns of tangible behavior that is organized around a set of coherent interests or social conditions or both. It is explained and justified by a set of related values, attitudes, and orientations and, under certain conditions, becomes the basis for a separate, common social identity for its participants. (Stebbins, 1997b, p. 350)

A profound lifestyle awaits anyone who routinely pursues a serious leisure career in, say, amateur theater, volunteer work with the mentally handicapped, the hobby of model railroading, or that of mountain climbing. It is also possible that this person finds exciting, albeit clearly less profound, lifestyles in casual leisure pastimes such as socializing in hot tubs and "whooping it up" at weekend beer parties. Many other forms of casual leisure, such as routine people watching and strolling in the park, are usually not shared with large numbers of other people, and therefore cannot be considered lifestyles according to the preceding definition. Moreover, in themselves, these activities are too superficial and unremarkable to serve as the basis for a recognizable mode of living.

In this definition of lifestyle it is, in particular, the shared patterns of tangible behavior that are of interest in this book since leisure lifestyles vary in significant part by the timing of activities that take place in each type of leisure organization. For example, two friends can schedule their racquetball matches around their personal routines and the availability of courts where they play. Many volunteers have similar flexibility in executing their responsibilities. By contrast members of sports and arts organizations holding regular practices and rehearsals must conform to event schedules set for the general convenience of all, which means some individuals will inevitably be inconvenienced. Furthermore, some leisure organizations do not meet at all. As will become evident later, social networks, social movements, and social worlds are diffuse, abstract entities that provide a special context for "acting" organizations of people to get together to pursue certain leisure interests. Social networks, social movements, and the like do not act by themselves.

The point here is that, in attempting to understand what moves people to adopt certain forms of leisure and associated lifestyles rather than others, we must always remember to consider the appeal of organizational routine. Temporal structuring of leisure is in large part determined by the participant.

At the very least this person can reject a leisure activity because its schedule is unappealing, it conflicts with certain obligations or cherished leisure activities, or it is too time-consuming. Of course, some people have leisure lifestyles that function independent of organizations, as is true for many lone-wolf hobbyists in, for instance, collecting, making and tinkering, and the liberal arts. But when people become involved with an organization, no matter how small, they must start to consider the interests of other members and adjust their own allocation of time to some extent.

Optimal Leisure Lifestyle

This discussion of leisure organization as it relates to serious and casual leisure and leisure lifestyle brings up the question of how to optimize the latter. In defining optimal leisure lifestyle, it was observed that a person finds one by engaging in leisure activities that individually and in combination realize human potential and enhance quality of life and personal well-being. People seeking to optimize their leisure this way strive to get the best return they can from their use of free time. What is considered "best" is, of course, a matter of personal definition; quality of optimal leisure lifestyle is predicated on a person's awareness of the vast range of available leisure possibilities. Thus people know they have reached an optimal leisure lifestyle when, from their own reasonably wide knowledge of feasible serious and casual leisure activities and associated costs and rewards, they can say they have enhanced their free-time well-being to the fullest by having found the best combination of the two types of leisure.

A highly satisfying leisure life is predicated, in part, on a workable schedule of all leisure activities as well as involvement, where possible and desirable, in organizations having substantial appeal. Optimally, then, organized involvements will be temporally and geographically spaced in a way that participants avoid feeling pressed to get from one to another. Moreover, activities will be complementary. Thus, it is hardly optimal to schedule an enervating afternoon session of pickup basketball before an evening rehearsal of the local barbershop chorus, which will entail at least two hours of standing on risers accompanied by plenty of diaphragm work. Perhaps the most important fact is that organizations themselves are powerfully attractive, which includes the people in them, the way they conduct the leisure in question, and the places where it occurs.

Finding an optimal leisure lifestyle can only be a goal for people pursuing more than one leisure activity, which they do in the course of the usual divisions of time: week, month, season, and year. Many people, however, pursue these activities with the aid of a handful of organizations. The smallest of these is the small group.

Chapter Two

Small Groups and Social Networks

This chapter examines leisure organization as manifested in dyads, or inter-personal relationships, triads, and other small groups of somewhat larger size as well as within social networks. In sociological parlance dyads and triads are special variants of the small group, the latter being defined as

> [a collectivity] small enough for all members to interact simultaneously, to talk to each other or at least to be known to each other. Another requirement is a minimum conviction of belonging to the group, a distinction between "us," the members of the group, and "them," the nonmembers. (Back, 1981, p. 320)

Moreover, dyads and other small groups endure, although only rarely for the lifetime of their members. At the same time, they are anything but eva-nescent. A gathering of passersby on a street corner animatedly discussing an automobile accident, or two airplane passengers gabbing throughout the whole flight but going their separate ways upon disembarking does not make a small group.

Small groups, whatever their size, generate their own idiocultures, or distinctive sets of shared ideas that emerge with reference to them (Fine, 1979). *Idioculture* is local culture, developed within and as an expression of an actual small group. It consists of a system of knowledge, beliefs, behaviors, and customs peculiar to that collectivity. Members use this system when interacting with one another, and expect that they will be understood by other members.

Informal small groups have roles and goals which are often not clearly defined. Such groups are further held together by members' recognition of the group's distinction of being a group of accepted individuals to the ex-clusion of other people. In formal small groups, rules, roles, and goals are more or less explicit. Most groups, formal or informal, are established to attain an agreed-upon goal. For some formal groups this may require a legal charter or, at the very least, some sort of written or public recognition as a group. Specialists in group research classify a small group as any organized unit of two to twenty individuals; however, this classification is arbitrary. Nonetheless, whatever its numerical size, a group becomes "large" when regular interaction is substantially limited and intimacy between all members is no longer experienced; that is, the group becomes large when the amount and quality of intermember communication are diluted.

Dyads

Although the terms dyad and interpersonal relationship both refer to two-person groups, they emphasize different facets of it. The first points to numerical composition, while the second draws attention to the substantial level of intimacy and frequency of interaction existing between two people. Especially appealing in leisure dyads is the interpersonal component; each person through participating with the other in a given activity or set of activities gains a high level of deeply satisfying intimacy and interaction. This explains Kelly and Godbey's (1992, pp. 214–216) preference for describing leisure in small groups as "relational leisure."

It appears that a good deal of contemporary leisure is organized in dyads. Same-sex and opposite-sex partners pursue a huge variety of activities ranging from pairs who play golf together, collect something, or go ballroom dancing to those who meet routinely for drinks, fishing outings, or sessions of hiking, dining out, or making music. Many of these dyads are informal, but not all of them. Although rarely legally chartered, clear rules, roles, and goals structure the leisure behavior of pairs whose relationships are founded on regular racquetball matches, piano–violin duets, or games of chess, to mention a few of many activities that lend themselves well to more formal dyadic pursuit.

Although the matter has never been scientifically studied, it is quite possible that comparative research will show that casual leisure dyadic activities are likely to be informal whereas serious leisure activities are likely to be formal. Why? Because the criteria of formality—rules and roles and the goals sought using those rules and roles—suggest a need for an important degree of training in these organized activities. Indeed, this is the third distinguishing quality of serious leisure as described in the preceding chapter as significant personal effort based on specially acquired knowledge, training, or skill, and at times, all three.

In all these examples the interpersonal quality of the dyadic relationship helps explain the participants' motivation to engage in the leisure they share. It is not only that tennis is an interesting and challenging game or that sessions at the bar sometimes bubble with intrigue and gossip, but also that these highly attractive activities are undertaken by pairs of people who are close friends, spouses, or partners, where the personalities of each hold mutual magnetic appeal based on emotions and orientations such as love, trust, respect, and affection. Put in the more general terminology of the serious leisure perspective, captivating challenge, interest, intrigue, and the like which offer personal rewards, while gratifying interpersonal relations that offer social reward. Most pertinent here of the ten rewards is the eighth: social attraction (i.e., associating with other serious leisure participants, serving clients as a volunteer, participating in the social world of the activity).

Perhaps nowhere else is the capacity of the dyadic relationship to motivate leisure participation more evident than among people with disabilities. Aitchison (2000), in a study of British youth with disabilities, observed that the lack of opportunities to interact with friends and peers was a concern for both the youth and their parents. Who these youth associated with was more important than the leisure activities shared, or the places where the activities occurred.

With or without disabilities, one reason for placing high value on interpersonal relationships during leisure is that each generates its own idioculture. An idioculture consists of, among other things, a rudimentary common language, some common goals, and various memories of common experiences. Some of the language, goals, and experiences are those related to the mutual leisure pursuit, as seen in the shared culture of two friends who frequently ski or attend the theater together. Recognition of this special culture contributes to the perception of the relationship as unique among other relationships (us compared with them) (McCall & Simmons, 1978, pp. 174–175).

Despite the importance attributed to the dyad as organizational incentive to get people to take up and continue with particular leisure activities, comparatively little research has been conducted on it. Orthner (1975), in describing his three types of marital leisure, did recognize the existence of dyadic leisure. He discussed joint activities requiring interaction (e.g., a card game) vis-à-vis individual activities engaged in alone, and parallel activities requiring little interaction even though done together (e.g., watching a hockey game). Furthermore, research reveals that some serious leisure tends to exclude spouses (even though friendships may develop there), as was found for amateurs in theater and baseball, hobbyists in barbershop singing, and career volunteers in grassroots organizations (Stebbins, 1979,

1996a, 1998b). By contrast, amateurs in archaeology and astronomy do sometimes pursue these activities as leisure with their spouses (Stebbins, 1979, 1980). The following poem, written in response to another poem about marital discord in leisure, illustrates well many of the motivational properties inherent in leisure-based interpersonal relationships.

One Astronomer's Wife

I awake a few hours preceding the dawn
And find my astronomer-husband gone.
I bound out of bed—I cannot have this!
He's doubtless found something that I must not miss.

The moon, stars, and planets, the great nebulae,
Are worlds that my husband has opened for me.
Orion and Saturn are friends of us both,
Our telescope brings us a new means for growth.
What a wonderful thing has come into our life!

My husband, I note, is increasingly mine,
As together we go where the galaxies shine.
When he's perched upon Plato's precipitous rim,
He's not there alone—I accompany him.
At predawn and midnight, in front of our house,
I gaze into far distant space with my spouse;
And while at breakfast we both may be tired,
I'm elated in sharing new knowledge acquired.
Behold lucky me, an astronomer's wife!

—Mrs. Lorena M. Cole
(*Sky and Telescope*, 18 [1959]: 137)

Goff, Fick, and Oppliger (1997) examined the moderating effect of spousal support on the relationship between serious leisure and spousal perception of leisure-family conflict. Their research on American male and female runners revealed that, if these runners had spouses who ran, the spouses were more likely to support the respondents' running than if they had spouses who did not run. Family conflict is thus one possible cost of pursuing serious leisure, although such conflict is less likely to occur when couples share the same leisure passion (Goff, Fick & Oppliger, 1997; Stebbins, 1979). In harmony with this observation Baldwin, Ellis, and Baldwin (1999) discovered that couples who share interests and participate together in activities find greater marital satisfaction than when they engage in parallel or independent activities.

Marital satisfaction, both as goal and as experience, is obviously a powerful reason for seeking leisure through the conjugal dyad. Apropos of this generalization, Flora and Segrin (1998) concluded from their sample of romantics and friends that they valued joint activity most highly, as compared to parallel or individual activity, but only as long as good social skills and positive interpersonal orientations prevailed. This was most true for sessions of relaxation, however, and less so for leisure activity centered on a game or a television program.

Green (1998) examined the question of women's same-sex friendships. She discovered that talk is central to these links and to the sense of leisure they provide. In this, a type of casual leisure, they share intimacies, while avoiding at least some of the gender stereotyped roles and images that come with keeping mixed company. Additionally, this leisure often takes place in favored places, such as kitchens for women and, for girls, their bedrooms.

Lest one conclude from the poem and various observations presented in this section that life in leisure-based dyads is one of unalloyed bliss. Note that disagreements can certainly occur, even if, over the years, the general tenor of the relationship remains positive. Furthermore, it is not impossible that a pair may grow apart in their leisure pursuit, as for instance, when one of them tires of an activity or improves dramatically compared with the other. Family or work pressures can also force one or both members of a dyad to curtail involvement in the common leisure activity. Given the possibility that the leisure part of a relationship may sour, brings to the fore the need to view through the prism of time all leisure organizations, no matter how large or small.

Other Small Groups

The term *small group*, like that of dyad, tends to stress numerical composition, even though intimacy and frequency of interaction are quintessential interpersonal qualities found in both. As in the interpersonal relationship, individual members of small groups have, in most instances, positive emotional attachments to each other and are known to each other as whole personalities rather than as partial individuals filling specialized roles. Since leisure studies has yet to examine the triad as a distinctive unit of leisure organization and participation, it will not be further considered here. I wish to challenge researchers to begin exploring three-person friendships and family groups for the distinctive leisure dynamics that may exist there.

Nevertheless, other small leisure groups have been widely studied, most notably the nuclear family and the adolescent peer group. A sample of this voluminous literature as it bears on the scope of this book is reviewed in this section. We first turn to the family.

One broad observation emerges from research in this area that bears on the present discussion is family leisure changes over the family life cycle (e.g., Rapoport & Rapoport, 1978). In other words, leisure varies in amount as well as in quality, depending on among other conditions, presence of children, demands of work (both inside and outside the home), shifting free-time interests, and obligations of family caregiving (Brattain Rogers, 1999). Kelly notes further that

> complementary kinds of leisure that are related to primary roles are valued more highly because of satisfactions attached to those relationships. Family leisure may be more constrained by expectations, but also [may] be more satisfying…. It is not that we disvalue freedom, but that family interaction—even with somewhat less freedom—is valued more highly. For most adults, then, the most important leisure is relational, social leisure chosen because of the positive satisfactions anticipated. (1983, pp. 129–130)

Kelly goes on to observe that, in this group, family interaction is itself an important form of leisure, as manifested in such casual leisure activities as holding conversations, visiting kin, and playing with children.

Mindful of Kelly's comments about constraints, we must be careful here about interpreting just how "leisurely" these sessions are for all concerned. Horna (1994, pp. 86–87) observes that someone (usually mother or another woman) must organize the picnic or the extended family feast, and she may well define the entire affair as mostly a chore. Christmas can be, in this regard, especially hellish for mother and other females responsible for the culinary pleasures of the assembled extended family (Bella, 1992). Larson, Gillman, and Richards (1997) found in their sample of European-American lower-class and middle-class families that, in general, mother's role as the person primarily responsible for everyday care of children and family gives her less freedom, and makes it more difficult for her to enjoy family leisure. By contrast, father, in his traditional position as primary breadwinner, finds it easier to use family leisure for diversion and self-expression. Now compare this situation with the egalitarian partnership found in lesbian families, where family tasks are not allocated along traditional sex lines but rather are negotiated which leaves both women with equal amounts of free time for themselves, each other, and family as a whole (Bialeschki & Pearce, 1997).

Adolescent Groups

Adolescents, especially older ones, fit uneasily in the family leisure scene. Larson and his colleagues (1997), who reviewed much of the relevant literature in this area, concluded that family and even home leisure are often peripheral for them. Indeed, these authors cite research indicating that, when asked directly to discuss leisure preferences, most adolescents even fail to mention leisure activities with family. One study revealed that parents were more influential than peers or activity leaders only in persuading adolescents not to join an activity (Hultsman, 1993). Adolescents feel this influence through certain constraints imposed by parents, most prominently that the activity is too expensive, parents forbid participating in it, or they provide no transportation with which to reach it. Still, evidence from comparative research in Norway and the United States reveals that both parents and peers can become models for young adolescents to take up and continue particular physical activities (Anderssen & Wold, 1992). This study also showed that encouragement from one or both of these sources is certainly important.

Kelly (1983, p. 62) notes that "leisure roles may well be most central to working out the intimacy, peer acceptance, cohort identification, self-definitional, and independence tasks of adolescent development." Young people find opportunities in leisure to reinforce, affirm, and experiment with various roles. Larson, Gillman, and Richards (1997, p. 81) write that, vis-à-vis their parents, leisure has different functions for young adolescents. For instance, excitement is more important for the latter, in part as reaction to the boredom of school. Leisure also fills the function of meeting changing developmental needs in social interaction and relations with peers. Third, leisure is a vehicle by which adolescents establish important peer-valued identities. In this regard, parents typically crave less excitement, are unable to meet adolescent developmental needs as peers do, and often resist, if not directly discourage, adolescents' attempts to express individuality. These gaps between the two generations frequently result in conflict.

These three functions already say a great deal about the nature of adolescent peer groups. Through such groups adolescents express individuality in the teenage world by participating in like-minded collectivities organized along lines of taste in music, clothing, leisure activities, and the like. While some of their interests can be qualified as serious leisure, the large majority have been found to prefer casual leisure, often experienced through sociable conversation with others teens (Mannell & Kleiber, 1997, pp. 237–238). In this regard, females compared with males tend to prefer relaxation rather than action and challenge (Kleiber, Caldwell & Shaw, 1993).

Still, boredom, which is experienced in free time and not just in school, is a frequent complaint of adolescents. In free time, boredom is a constraint that inhibits people from experiencing leisure (Ragheb & Merydith, 2001, p. 43). Among its components are slowness of time, lack of meaningful involvement, and lack of mental and physical involvement. Shaw, Caldwell, and Kleiber (1996) found boredom is related not only to lack of attractive leisure outlets but also to participation in adult-structured activities. More-over, even teenage dyadic and larger group relationships fail to provide sure-fire antidotes to this dreary state of mind, while solitude, which many younger adolescents abhor in any case (Kleiber, 1999, pp. 48–49), offers no cure either.

Being bored helps explain the appeal of deviant leisure among a small proportion of today's adolescents (Stebbins, 1997a). Such leisure in this age category can also be traced to the young person's search for indepen-dence, although in this regard, it is unnecessary to defy the adult world to achieve it (Roberts, 1999, p. 119). Most deviant leisure, adolescent or oth-erwise, fits the description of tolerable deviance (Stebbins, 1996b).

Although contravention of certain moral norms of society as held by the majority of its members to be mildly threatening in most social situa-tions, tolerable deviance nevertheless fails to generate any significant or ef-fective communal attempts to control it (Stebbins, 1996b, pp. 3–4). Such deviance undertaken for pleasure—as casual leisure—encompasses a range of deviant sexual activities including cross-dressing, homosexuality, and watching sex (e.g., striptease, visual pornographic material) as well as swinging and group sex. Heavy drinking and gambling, but not their more seriously regarded cousins alcoholism and compulsive gambling, are also tolerably deviant and hence forms of casual leisure as are use of cannabis and illicit, pleasurable, use of certain prescription drugs. Social nudism has also been analyzed within the tolerable deviance perspective (all these forms are examined in greater detail in Stebbins, 1996b).

In the final analysis, deviant casual leisure is rooted in sensory stimula-tion and, in particular, the creature pleasures it produces. The majority of people in society tolerate most of these pleasures even if they would never think, or at least not dare, to enjoy themselves in these ways. In addition, they actively scorn a somewhat smaller number of intolerable forms of deviant casual leisure, demanding decisive police control of, for example, incest, vandalism, sexual assault, and what Jack Katz (1988) calls "sneaky thrills" (certain acts of theft, burglary, shoplifting, and joyriding). Sneaky thrills, however, are motivated not by desire for creature pleasure but rather by desire for a special kind of excitement: going against the grain of established community norms without getting caught.

Adolescents of both sexes have found collective leisure in the majority of these forms of deviance, albeit always as a minority of all adolescents and in numbers that vary by sex and age. In a study composed of male and female homosexuals, Caldwell, Kivel, Smith, and Hayes (1998) learned that, compared with heterosexual peers, boredom in free-time was an incentive to engage in higher levels of binge drinking, and Jankowski describes the recreational appeal of gangs as an escape from boredom for late adolescents and young men:

> The gang provides individuals with entertainment, much as
> a fraternity does for college students or the Moose and Elk
> Clubs do for their members. Many individuals said they
> joined the gang because it was the primary social institution
> of their neighborhood—that is, it was where most (not nec-
> essarily the biggest) social events occurred. Gangs usually,
> though not always, have some type of clubhouse....Every
> clubhouse offers some form of entertainment. (Jankowski,
> 1999, pp. 276–277)

Additionally, some clubhouses have bars, while others are furnished with pool tables, pinball machines, or card tables. Gangs may hold parties and dances, thus providing male members with the opportunity to meet women. Some are sources of drugs. In short, gangs help adolescents (and young men) deal with boredom.

Like adults, only a small portion of all adolescents seem to become enamored of one or more serious leisure pursuits, and only a portion of these join or establish an organization for this purpose. This area badly needs empirical study. Nevertheless, it is evident that some adolescents do become members of, for example, small music ensembles, sports teams, hobbyist groups, or volunteer service units. Here, in contrast to their casual leisure pursuits, they typically participate through specialized roles that together make a larger whole, such as performing a jazz tune or playing a basketball game. Here, too, personal identity hinges not only on group membership but also on how well individuals carry out their roles. Thus membership in a serious leisure group, unlike that in a casual leisure group, brings recognition for the acquired skills, knowledge, and experience needed to execute the activity in question well.

Furthermore, it appears that most small groups of serious leisure participants are organized and directed by youth themselves rather than by adults. This is as youth would have it. For with youth, adult direction is typically too constraining and heavy handed. In keeping with earlier definitions, such groups do endure, however. Sociologically speaking they amount to more than jazz musicians "blowing" tunes at a jam session or basketball players working up a sweat in a pickup game.

Adult Groups

Whatever the reason, adult small leisure groups have attracted rather less research attention than family and adolescent leisure groups (Scott & Godbey, 1992, p. 48). To be sure, many adult groups have escaped notice because they are informal units that have emerged within larger clubs, associations, societies, and the like (e.g., those who regularly golf, bowl, or dine out together). Yet, some exist as independent entities such as small sets of amateur athletes, musicians, and entertainers as well as small clubs of hobbyists. What is the nature of research in this area?

On the hobbyist scene, Scott and Godbey (1992) examined a sample of four contract bridge clubs, which met regularly to play, three of which could be classified as small groups (consisting of nine to twelve players). The authors found that some clubs approached the game as a social activity (casual leisure) whereas others approached it as serious leisure. The typical social bridge club recruits by invitation and by personal compatibility with existing members. Its primary function is to strengthen interpersonal ties within the club, which meets in players' homes. When together, members chat about work, friends, and family. On the other hand, the typical serious club, given its primary function of providing opportunities to play bridge, recruits openly according to ability. Games commonly take place at the club's facility, where talk tends to center on bridge strategy and bridge stories. Serious clubs are members of the American Contract Bridge League; social clubs are not.

Fine studied role-playing or fantasy games defined as

> any game which allows a number of players to assume the roles of imaginary characters and operate with some degree of freedom in an imaginary environment. (1983, p. 6)

His study of this hobby included participant observation at a couple of clubs, where he noted that strong friendships develop around a gaming culture created by their members through shared gaming experiences. Interpersonal relations in the clubs consisted in part of teasing, whereby one member would attempt to depreciate another by referring to the foolishness of the character that person was presenting (Fine, 1983, pp. 137–142).

Curling teams, which are four-person units, exhibit considerable internal specialization along lines of certain social, technical, and psychological skills expected for each position (Apostle, 1992). The lead, the first to throw the two rocks allotted each player, should be a quiet, stable person who can provide calm, stability, and mature reflection when a game is progressing poorly. By contrast, the skip, the last to throw the rocks, is expected to be the best person in the group for handling pressure and providing personal leadership. Additionally, the team as a whole must be tolerant of individual deficiencies and personal foibles in its members.

Mitchell (1983) writes about mountain climbing teams (hobbyist small groups), observing that cooperation in carrying out various duties and privileges (e.g., hauling loads, leading the ascent) is "a prime requisite in selecting companions." Moreover, in smaller groups individual affability is absolutely critical. The author concludes that

> companions, particularly in small groups on major climbs, find that their interdependence during long planning periods and on the mountain itself cements casual acquaintances into firm and lasting bonds. (pp. 16–17)

With each climber being dependent on the judgment and competence of the others, trust becomes a key orientation of group members toward one another.

Another genre of trust is evident in accepting or rejecting as true claimed achievements of people in leisure pursuits. Donnelly (1994) examined this relationship in mounting climbing and bird-watching. In both activities, a stranger purporting to have climbed a difficult peak, climbed a more easily reachable peak using a difficult route, or seen a rare bird is subject to a set of verificational questions from experienced participants in the field who have learned to be suspicious of such claims. From the standpoint of leisure motivation, such scrutiny protects participants from establishing relationships with other participants of dubious competence in and commitment to the activity they share.

Singing in a barbershop quartet stands as another collective hobby on which research has been conducted. Weekly rehearsals, critical evaluations, and various public concerts bring together in many interpersonally significant ways these small groups of men or women (Stebbins, 1996a, p. 51). For example, given their close and intense interaction, all participants must be able to get along with each other. They must also agree on goals for their quartet. For example, should they stick to giving occasional local concerts, or strive for national recognition achieved by participating in formal competitions? Above all, they must have an acceptable blend of voices and be prepared to devote the time needed to reach their shared goals. Close friendships typically develop over the course of all this.

Social Networks

The definition of social network that best fits the small amount of work done on this form of organization within the domain of leisure is that of Elizabeth Bott. Her definition is simple: a social network is "a set of social relationships for which there is no common boundary" (1957, p. 59). In the strict sense of the word, a network is not a structure, since it has no shared boundaries (i.e., boundaries recognized by everyone in the social network) and no commonly recognized hierarchy or central coordinating agency. Nevertheless, interconnections exist between others in the network, in that some members are directly in touch with each other while others are not. Thus it is also true of networks that their mesh may be "closely-knit" (i.e., many members having direct contact) or "loosely-knit" (i.e., few members having direct contact) (Barnes, 1954; Bott, 1957, p. 59). As for their size, many social networks are no larger than most small groups, although some are so large and extensive that they span regional or national boundaries.

Over the years, social networks have been analyzed from two basic approaches. One—that of Bott—is ego-centered, the view of the network of a particular individual who is part of it. The other is holistic; here the component relationships are seen as the sum of every individual's personal network. Both approaches are relevant for explaining participation in leisure as analyzed from an organizational framework. The first, which is the more common network analyses in leisure studies, examines the structure of social interaction, starting with the relationships one person maintains with others in that person's network, defined as "points," and then tracing those relationships as "lines" connecting the points.

As individuals pursue their leisure interests, they develop networks of contacts (friends and acquaintances) related in one way or another to these interests. As a person develops more interests, the number of networks grows accordingly, bearing in mind that members of some of these may overlap. For instance, a few members of John's dog breeding network—they might be suppliers, veterinarians, or other breeders—are also members of his golf network—who might be suppliers, course personnel, or other golfers. Knowing about people's leisure networks helps explain how they organize their leisure time socially. In this manner, as Blackshaw and Long (1998, p. 246) point out, we learn something new about leisure lifestyle.

The importance of social networks for generating leisure opportunities and motivating people to take advantage of them is evident in Hibbler and Shinew's (2002) research. They found in their study of American interracial couples that the couples' social networks were unusually limited—a condition that tended to restrict their leisure involvement. In those parts of the United States where Black-White marriages are frowned upon, couples thus constituted face discrimination and rejection for this reason. As a result they have comparatively fewer friends and acquaintances, which in turn, truncates their opportunities to participate in leisure outside their family circle.

In a rare study of leisure networks, Stebbins (1976) examined those of amateur classical musicians. One analytic characteristic of social networks is their reachability, which denotes in a person's network the number of intermediaries who must be contacted to reach certain others in it. Reachability is relatively great when few or no intermediaries are needed for this purpose, as opposed to when many are needed. Thus, in a community orchestra, the concertmaster usually has greater reachability than any other instrumentalist in the ensemble, because of responsibilities demanding direct contact with the majority of its members. For example, this person may be simultaneously assistant conductor, chief recruiter and disciplinarian, all in addition to being the orchestra's subleader. Extensive reachability is crucial for effective functioning of people in this role. Consequently, it is difficult to urge better intonation, consistent punctuality at rehearsals, and greater artistic playing from a musician with whom the concertmaster has no direct relationship.

In the field of leisure studies, Patricia Stokowski has devoted by far the most attention to the question of social networks (see Stokowski, 1994, for an overview of her contributions). She and a colleague (Stokowski & Lee, 1991) mounted an exploratory study guided by Bott's ego-centered concept, the purpose of which was to demonstrate the utility of this approach. Among the questions explored was one concerning strength of network ties. She found that people tend to engage in leisure with significant others, and people with whom they have strong ties. Still, some respondents had strong ties only with immediately family, while their ties with extended family and friends were weak. People with leisure networks of this sort were located on the periphery of the community as a whole as well as on the periphery of its visible activities. By contrast, respondents with strong ties to immediate family and at least moderately strong ties to either extended family or good friends were involved in a much broader range of more central activities.

Conclusions

Personal interest in certain free-time activities, individuated patterns of leisure lifestyle, and intensive participation in related leisure organizations, including those just considered, together constitute a substantial explanation of leisure motivation. In trying to pursue a particular leisure interest, the individual soon finds that time and space have become structured in particular ways, which includes routine, if not regular, interaction with certain people in organizations. Put otherwise, tangible patterns of behavior emerge, which are appealing in part because they are social. To the extent that no other available interest can produce a more satisfying or enjoyable return during free time, this lifestyle, or more precisely, this part of the person's overall leisure lifestyle, can be described as optimal.

The question now is how do larger, more formal groups fit this motivational model? Of these, grassroots associations are most similar to these small groups.

Chapter Three
Grassroots Associations

Although no one knows precisely the proportion, a substantial amount of all leisure takes place, partly or wholly, in grassroots associations. When leisure studies looks carefully at this question, its researchers will learn that only the form of leisure organization considered in Chapter 6, the social world, rivals the grassroots association as the most common way of collectively pursuing free-time activities. Still, for all its importance, the latter has not been directly examined to any great extent to date, either in leisure studies or in voluntary action research. To be sure, there has been both theoretical and empirical work in this area, but it will become apparent in this chapter that much remains to be done. Indeed, the term grassroots association is a neologism of recent origin.

Definition and Description

Possibly no earlier than 1997, David Horton Smith (e.g., Smith, 1997) began referring to a special type of voluntary association that other scholars in voluntary action research were generally inclined to ignore as *grassroots association*. His terminological invention was neither an accident nor an attempt to pour old wine into a new bottle. For as a scientific concept, the related idea of voluntary association is cumbersome in diverse ways—it masks numerous distinctions of great import to scholars interested in social organization of leisure and how such an organization influences collective social life and motivates individual participation.

Although Smith briefly defines grassroots associations as local volunteer groups, this shorthand omits several important criteria that further demarcate them. Much more informative, then, is his expanded "connotative" definition:

> Grassroots associations are locally based, significantly au-
> tonomous, volunteer-run formal nonprofit (i.e., voluntary)
> groups that manifest substantial voluntary altruism as groups,
> and use the associational form of organization and, thus,
> have official memberships of volunteers who perform most,
> and often all, of the work/activity done in and by these
> nonprofits. (Smith, 2000, p. 8)

The term *formal* in this definition refers in fact to a scale of structure and operations that in an actual association may be informal, semiformal, or formal. Moreover, the line separating grassroots associations from paid-staff voluntary groups—treated in the next chapter as volunteer organizations—is unavoidably fuzzy; it being primarily a matter of gradation. Both types fall under the heading of *voluntary groups*: "nonprofit groups of any type, whether grassroots associations or based on paid staff, and whether local, national, or international in scope" (Smith, 2000, p. ix).

Lengkeek and Bargeman (1997, p. 238) see the collective world much as Smith does, distinguishing what they call simply "organizations," collectivities established by nonparticipants for certain kinds of participants (e.g., a sports team for children, a social center for the elderly), from those founded by their own members, referred to above as grassroots associations. They go on to note that, among the latter, it is also necessary to identify those operating for others (e.g., a group of high school students formed to welcome new students) from those working for themselves (e.g., self-help groups, clubs formed to facilitate pursuit of a hobby or an amateur science).

Furthermore, some grassroots associations are *monomorphic*. These constitute unique local entities, such as a community theater, club for women, or society for welcoming newcomers (Smith, 2000, p. 117). Other associations are *polymorphic*, similar in form to a number of sister associations, where each is affiliated with a larger, overarching organization. Examples of this type include local units of Rotary International, the Society for the Preservation and Encouragement of Barbershop Quartet Singing in America (SPEBSQSA), and the Canadian Intercollegiate Athletic Union, which organizes various male and female university sports teams.

Common to all types of voluntary groups is the condition that a significant proportion of participating members are motivated by voluntary altruism. What is voluntary altruism? Altruism is regard for others as a basis for action with reference to them—an act of unselfishness. According to Smith (2000, pp. 19–20) it is voluntary when there is (1) a mix of human caring and sharing of oneself and one's resources; (2) at least a moderate freedom to chose the activity; (3) a lack of coercion from biopsychic, biosocial, or socially compulsive forces; (4) a sensitivity to certain needs and wants of a target population; (5) an expectation of little or no remuneration or payment in kind; and (6) an expectation of receiving some kind of satisfaction for action undertaken with reference to a target population. This sixth component of voluntary altruism is consistent with the observation that two principal motives are actually operating when it is expressed: one is helping others—volunteering as unselfishness—and the other is helping oneself—volunteering as self-interestedness (Stebbins, 1996c, p. 213).

Lest this observation appear contradictory, bear in mind that self-interested behavior is only selfish when it unfairly exploits someone else (Stebbins, 1993b, p. 51). Nevertheless, the commonsense idea that volunteering is essentially altruistic fails to square with reality. For instance, Harris writes that

> the difficulty of ensuring that volunteer members carry out essential organizational tasks is compounded by the fact that members seem largely motivated to take on voluntary work within associations because of the opportunities it provides for autonomy, self-fulfillment, and expressive relationships. Thus, they do not generally expect to be managed, controlled, monitored, or subjected to the norms of hierarchical bureaucratic structures. To the extent that they see themselves as being directed or overridden, the commitment of member volunteers can melt away. (1998, p. 151)

Indeed, as will be discussed in more detail later, self-interested motives sometimes rattle organizational life in storms of conflict of varying magnitude, originating in discordant goals among individual members or in goals of a group of them that clash with those of the larger collectivity.

For all the talk about volunteers and voluntariness in Smith's conceptualization, these two ideas are nonetheless broad enough to include organized amateurs and hobbyists (e.g., Smith, 2000, p. 248), serious leisure participants described in Chapter 1 as separate types from career volunteers. As stated elsewhere (Stebbins, 1992, p. 16), altruism motivates all these participants. But whereas it is a main motive among career volunteers, it is a secondary one among amateurs and hobbyists. Indeed, as Hoggett and Bishop (1985) observed with a sample of British hobbyist groups

> we found no sense of an involvement in *voluntary* organizations, and very few people who would accept that their involvement in their group constitutes any form of *volunteering*. Indeed, some would vehemently deny that they are "volunteers." (p. 24)

Yet, a few pages later these same authors note that people appear to recognize the need to harmonize, we would say here, quite altruistically, their aspirations with the culture of the group (p. 29). In a word, they try to fit in. Thus it will be useful in this chapter, as in earlier ones, to underscore from time to time the importance of self-interestedness as a motive for pursuing a hobby or an amateur activity, while doing the same for the motive of altruism when volunteering is considered. Grassroots associations are formed in response to both dispositions and, once established, help channel them.

Leisure Grassroots Associations

By distinguishing volunteer organizations from grassroots associations, Smith clears the way for discussion of the leisure basis of the second (e.g., Smith, 2000, pp. 11–12). We will see in Chapter 4 that volunteer organizations, though they rely significantly on volunteer help, are not established for pursuing a pastime. Not so with grassroots associations. In various ways many of them come into existence to foster one or more forms of casual or serious leisure, springing up in nearly every sphere of life.

The range of grassroots associations appears to encompass all 16 areas of service provided by career volunteers (described in Chapter 1). It is also evident that amateurs and hobbyists often pursue their leisure in some of these areas, notably in health, science, and spiritual development, as well as in religion, recreation, human relationships, and the arts. Moreover, as noted in the preceding chapter, some serious and casual leisure is deviant. Smith (in press) observes that grassroots associations are occasionally founded precisely to facilitate such activity. It would be ideal were we able to examine the motivational aspects of organizational participation in both deviant and nondeviant casual and serious leisure. But this is not for the present book, since empirical work is in short supply in this field.

Smith's (2000, pp. 95–105) review of the literature does uncover, however, a sizeable list of important generalizations about the motivational appeal of involvement in grassroots associations. Altruism and self-interestedness, in diverse combinations, are the basic motives here, of course, but other secondary motives, like all motives, also initiate, pattern, time, and direct action. Smith refers these as "incentives." Most important among them are the sociability and purposive incentives. The first refers to satisfaction members receive from being in the company of and interacting with other members and clients of the association and from friendships and acquaintanceships that develop along the way. Purposive incentives bring satisfaction through realizing the group's goals, achieved in ways consonant with its ideology about what the goals should be and how to reach them.

Smith goes on to consider seven other incentives that motivate people to participate in grassroots associations, participation depending on the nature of the group and the needs of individual members. Service incentives are of two kinds: helping clients (e.g., delivering suppers for Meals-On-Wheels) or helping other members (e.g., playing a musical instrument in the local civic orchestra). Informational incentives are at work when people join an association to gain knowledge about something, as in belonging to a computer club or an amateur science society. People seeking personal growth have a developmental incentive for seeking membership in certain grassroots associations. For instance, they may be trying to "resist" stereotyped images of people like themselves as female, elderly, or handicapped (see Shaw, 2001) or hoping to use a self-help group to better the situation of their own kind.

Some members of these organizations join for a utilitarian reason—their motive is material, remunerative, or occupational. For others it is professional or economic. Opportunities provided by the group for making business contacts (as in the various service and business clubs), getting an inside line on a job, or obtaining free passes to artistic events exemplify this incentive. The charismatic incentive helps explain why a person joins a grassroots association to be led by or associate with a highly attractive and influential personality. Religious cults, for example, often gain adherents by this means. Akin to the purposive incentive is the lobbying incentive, expressed in advocacy and representation to government. Usually, however, such activity takes place on a regional or national plane, well beyond the scope of the typical local group. Last on the list although hardly least, is the prestige incentive. It is an honor to be a member, and even more honorable to be an officer, of an exclusive organization such as one of the city's elite country clubs or business organizations.

Participatory Features

Several features of life in grassroots associations further account for participation there. Bishop and Hoggett (1986), in an extensive study of amateur and hobbyist groups in two communities in England, identified three:

leisure subcultures, contributions of individual members, and handling member diversity. We turn first to the matter of subcultures.

The subculture of grassroots associations is the analog of the idioculture of small groups (described in the preceding chapter), and in fact, when associations are of small group size, the two are, in this respect, one and the same. For the associational subculture is also local, developed within and as an expression of an actual collectivity. It, too, consists of a system of knowledge, beliefs, behaviors, and customs peculiar to the group. Members use this system when interacting with one another, and expect for this reason to be understood by the others. Knowing the subculture and using it as interactive code is enjoyable in itself, still another reason for being in the group and pursuing activities it organizes.

Likewise there are group rules, values, and language, about which Hoggett and Bishop also wrote. Stebbins's (1993, pp. 58–63) study of amateur Canadian football players provides an illustration of these elements of culture. The norms of football include arriving on time at practices and games, coming there free of effects of alcohol and other recreational drugs, and showing commitment to the sport by running to and from assignments. A cardinal value for these players is winning the games they play, with playing well in each one being nearly as important. Moreover, the game of football is rich in special terms, a number of which denote technical matters: plays, skills, movements, and situations. Other terms are imperative; they are used to express a command such as "suck it up!" (be tough, work hard), "huddle up!" "get into the game!" (concentrate on playing football), and "listen up!" (be quiet and listen to the coach or other authority).

Contributions

To some extent, we have already considered the contributions individuals make to grassroots associations when we examined their incentives for joining them. That is, someone joining a group in search of sociability contributes to this side of group life while realizing a main personal goal. Similarly, a person who likes the services an organization offers—for instance maintaining hiking trails or conducting guided tours of an old church—contributes to it by helping provide those services. Possibly nowhere else in the vast world of leisure and voluntary action is the mesh of personal and collective interests so finely interwoven. Possibly nowhere else are the motives of altruism and self-interestedness so closely linked.

Still, Harris (1998, pp. 147–148) and Hoggett and Bishop (1985, p. 28), among others, point out that an incompatibility of goals sometimes arises; individuals may have aspirations that only a different grassroots association can help them fulfill. Factions may develop, with certain privileges and practices being jealously guarded in the face of opposition to them. Thus, a small number of male singers in the main barbershop chorus in the Canadian city of Calgary found it offered too little challenge for their singing abilities. They solved this problem by leaving the main group to form a more elite chorus of their own, whose approach to their hobby was more in line with their considerable singing talent (Stebbins, 1996a, p. 69). It was also true that some men left, or failed to join, the main chorus because, for them, it was too "serious." To sing choral music in a less demanding atmosphere, they would have to find a local church choir with which to perform. In general, however, "people appear to accept a need for balance between their aspirations and the dynamic of the group, therefore open definitions leave space for modification" (Hoggett & Bishop, 1985, p. 29).

This works, in part, because members of grassroots associations share a common identity, as people with similar distinctive goals and interests united under the same organizational banner. Apparently, a combination of tolerance for difference, respect for the goals being pursued, and love of the principle activity, among other criteria, help sustain a strong identification with the group for most members. Yet, there is more to it than this.

The work, or more accurately, the nonwork situation of many people in the present-day information age will consist, in part, of being cast adrift from the key organizational moorings of their employment days—a clear sign of a "post-traditional existence" (Stebbins, 1996d). More and more these people will find themselves floating, with no rudder, in an organizationless sea, a result of their unemployment, retirement, or marginal affiliation with a work organization as a temporary consultant or limited-term contractual worker. This absence of organizational ties will likely pose little or no problem for some people; their family relationships and friendship networks are all they will ever want. Others, however, may well miss the sense of belonging to a collectivity with greater public visibility and integration than networks and relationships typically have. If upon further research this proposition turns out to be true, being cut off from the organizational belongingness they once enjoyed at work will inspire these former employees to search for other organizations capable of replacing this loss. Enter the grassroots association as complementary organization (see Chapter 1).

Handling Diversity

As alluded to already, members of grassroots associations are in fact a diverse lot, not withstanding their common identity. The preceding discussion about different levels of talent among barbershop singers raises a parallel question about different levels of motivation to pursue personal and group goals. People whom I referred to earlier as *participants* routinely participate in the association and its principal leisure activity; in serious leisure, they are the ordinary amateurs, hobbyists, and volunteers themselves. By contrast, *devotees* are those among them who show exceptional devotion to the association and its activity, to maintaining it, to advancing it (Stebbins, 1992, pp. 46–48). Beyond these two types lie the multitude of dabblers, neophytes, and others only superficially involved in their activities. These are enjoying various kinds of casual leisure.

Officers in grassroots association were most likely to be members with the commitment of devotees. One might think such diversity of rank in an organization of equals (except for participant–devotee differences) might spawn resentment, jealousy, anxiety, and other divisive sentiments. Hoggett and Bishop's (1985, p. 34) research suggests, however, that it is generally the contrary, a conclusion that harmonizes with my own after examining amateurs and their organizations in archaeology, astronomy, baseball, and football as well as theater, classical music, entertainment magic, and grassroots volunteering among Canadian francophones. In the world of leisure a rudimentary democracy prevails at this level of organization, founded on official sensitivity to needs and wants of the rank-and-file (made possible by the fact that there are relatively few of them) as well as on the tendency to control intake of members. That is, grassroots groups have mechanisms, some more implicit than explicit, by which they screen potential newcomers. People who fail to fit because they are too good, too bad, or have the wrong attitude are simply rejected or, more indirectly, subtly discouraged from joining.

Provisioning Leisure

Gary Fine (1989) has sketched a theory of provisioning leisure, which underscores the importance of key resources for undertaking particular free-time activities. These resources are provided by organizations of every sort. Individual interest in a given activity, he observes, depends as much on it being available and having a reputation of being fun as on personal need and preference.

Fine sets out eight assumptions on which his theory rests, each based on the broad presupposition that most leisure organizations wish to grow and, at the very least, maintain a steady existence.

1. Organizations with greater access to resources will be more successful than those with less access to resources.

2. The extent of participation in leisure organizations depends on the organization's ability to provide desired resources for members.

3. Those organizations that provide the most resources to individual members will be those that succeed.

4. Leisure organizations compete in a market, and those that are more efficient in providing resources will survive better that those that are not.

5. Leisure organizations must make their activities known to a general public; those that publicize themselves most effectively will be most likely to survive. Effective leisure organizations connect themselves to media outlets and forms of interpersonal recruitment.

6. Individuals participating in a leisure activity must have access to credible information. Those organizations that are best able to provide this information will survive.

7. Individuals participating in a leisure activity must enjoy their relations with other participants. Those organizations that are best able to facilitate this sociability will survive.

8. Individuals participating in a leisure activity need their own personal identity validated. Those organizations that are best able to provide for identity validation will survive. (Fine, 1989, pp. 322–323)

Not every leisure organizations wants to grow or grow at the same rate, but each wants to survive, notwithstanding a small number of members who might prefer it be disbanded.

Fine also discusses four key resources of leisure organizations. One is knowledge, information that enables competent execution of the leisure activity. The second is sociability, and many clubs offer "sociable times" during a typical year, including dinners, picnics, parties, and receptions (e.g., weekly meetings of local Rotary chapters). Additionally, successful organizations allow time for informal interaction among members when attending meetings and other get-togethers. Many leisure activities have their identity symbols, something associated organizations can often provide, whether a cap, T-shirt, lapel pin, or bumper sticker. In prestigious organizations, the membership card is a primary identity symbol. Fourth, some leisure resources are copyrighted and made available only through an organization, as is true for barbershop music arrangements and guidebooks of hiking clubs.

Amateur Grassroots Associations

Mushroom collectors and mountain climbers number among the amateurs and hobbyists who often join small associations to better pursue their leisure passion. Fine and Holyfield (1996) explored the necessity for secrecy and trust of expert knowledge among these two kinds of enthusiasts, special relationships best cultivated in a group setting. In the course of being socialized to their serious leisure group, new members learned early in their careers as amateurs or hobbyists that they can trust the experts, but must not make public any information they gain from them. For example, secrecy prevents the public from learning about coveted mushrooming terrain or, in alpinism, favorite routes to difficult summits.

In some activities organizational membership facilitates amateur-professional contact and mutual respect across this work-leisure divide. In this regard, Taylor (1995) found that amateur archaeologists have gained a respected place in the vocabulary of their professional counterparts, contradicting the evolutionary model that depicts the former as eventually supplanted by the latter. Similarly, Baldwin and Norris's (1999) research on dog breeders and trainers in the American Kennel Club revealed that here, too, amateurs are reasonably well-integrated with professionals. These studies suggest that, whereas leisure marginality often exists in other parts of an amateur's life, in a few fields when it comes to relations with professionals, it is significantly diluted.

This is also true in entertainment magic, where both amateurs and professionals mix as members or, in the case of the former, as guest speakers for amateur audiences:

> For many amateurs and a smaller number of professionals, the Society of American Magicians and the International Brotherhood of Magicians are most meaningful at the local level where the monthly meetings and other activities of the ring or assembly occur....At the local meetings....there are opportunities for additional performing experience, for exchanging ideas and information on the art and business of magic, for hearing lectures from local and visiting specialists, and for discussing new tricks as well as the construction and modification of old ones. This, too, is where the various ethical precepts [of performance magic] become a reality for neophytes. The importance of living by them and citing cases where magicians either have failed to do so or have done so

exceptionally well drift in and out of the formal and informal proceedings of these meetings. (Stebbins, 1993c, p. 17)

Local meetings also offer good opportunities for screening out people wanting access to organized magic for reasons inimical to the art, such as to learn tricks they can then expose in print.

Hobbyist Grassroots Associations

Olmsted (1993) describes two hobbies organized in grassroots fashion heretofore ignored in leisure studies: dollhouse building and model railroading. From interviews with Canadian and American hobbyists, he learned that both activities are highly satisfying, in part because they enable participants to work alone. But he also found that each has its social side with its own special appeal. This is seen in the many small, formally or informally organized, local clubs, which meet regularly in members' homes. Larger, community-wide clubs, which enroll many members of the small clubs, organize shows, hold workshops, circulate newsletters, among other activities and services.

Another craft with no prior history of scientific study and one that knows no professional counterpart—though there is a commercial side—is quilting. King (1997) surveyed members of four local guilds in North Texas, where levels of commitment to and depth of knowledge of this hobby are significantly higher than among "casual" quilters (dabblers), who work alone at home. The hobbyists offered several reasons for quilting: it gives a sense of pride, expresses one's creativity, and provides opportunities to meet like-minded participants. For the most part the latter goal can only be reached by joining a guild, where members exchange ideas and technical information as well as collaborate on collective projects.

Moving to the realm of activity participation, Hamilton-Smith (1993) reports on the first exploration of "bushwalking," the Australian equivalent in other countries of hiking or backpacking. In Australia many participants in this hobby pursue it collectively through hiking clubs, doing so within a special cultural framework, or ethos, that rests on a belief in the rugged self-sufficient bushman and a desire for enhanced social standing that emulating this type can bring the walker. The appeal of social camaraderie during a group hike is obvious, even if the bushman type of hiker is disappearing, increasingly displaced by commercialized leisure services and opportunities.

More and more today, for example, a professional guide assumes the roles of cook, map reader, and expert locator of good campsites.

The study of Canadian male and female barbershop singers mentioned earlier (Stebbins, 1996a) constitutes a rare look at polymorphic grassroots associations. Local choruses in several countries around the world are affiliated with a national body, which among its many functions, sets performance standards, establishes organizational structure, holds annual conventions, and provides training information. Two such bodies in North America are the aforementioned SPEBSQSA and Sweet Adelines International.

This study revealed that personal enrichment was the most powerful reward in barbershop singing. It comes through the experience of performing—mainly in presenting a polished show or selection of songs before an appreciative audience—wherein the performer is swallowed up in a sea of barbershop song. That is, when the experience is enriching, he or she is surrounded by pure, ringing, consonant harmonies (the hallmark of barbershop) to which the audience avidly responds. Somewhat less powerful, though hardly insignificant, were the rewards of social attraction of the barbershop chorus and group accomplishment within it. The latter involved working with other members to produce ringing barbershop chords, good annual shows, and competitive ensembles for the next regional or national contest.

Volunteer Grassroots Associations

The study of volunteer grassroots associations brings to the fore the fact that for organizations, as for individuals, both costs and rewards must be considered to reach a truly full understanding of volunteer motivation. In this vein, Jarvis and King (1997) interviewed a sample of volunteers serving in Scout and Guide organizations in England. They found that a main reason for volunteering in them was to experience enjoyment from working with children and youth, a situation these groups made possible by bringing clients and volunteers together to participate in common projects. Their respondents gave work or family commitments as principal reasons for leaving the Guides and Scouts, suggesting that some of the most poignant costs of this leisure come as pressures external to it.

Arai (1997) observed in her research that voluntary action and the environment in which it is carried out are presently undergoing momentous change, and that empowerment theory can help us understand this change as it bears on volunteers and volunteering. To this end, Arai explored the relationship between empowerment, volunteering, and serious leisure, examining not only the benefits of these two pursuits for self and community, but also their undesirable or "dark" side, that is their costs. She concluded that, while volunteering often takes the form of serious leisure, we must nevertheless be sure to examine the negative implications of this kind of activity, which include certain tensions and power relationships that emerge at both the personal and the community levels.

Other Leisure

Not all serious leisure can be so neatly classified as has been done to this point. Indeed, in at least one field, mixed serious leisure appears to be the norm. That field is historical reenactment. Mittelstaedt (1995) observed in his study of Americans reenacting the Civil War that they are first of all amateur historians. However, when they present "living history" before an audience, these historians must also serve as amateur actors. Furthermore, to ensure realism, some enthusiasts go on to become makers of such items as horseshoes and laundry soap, items in use at the time but no longer available today in the same form (Mittelstaedt, 1990/91). A similar multiplicity of roles is evident in Revolutionary War reenactments (McKim, 1997) and, presumably, in the activities of the Society of Creative Anachronism, an international organization dedicated to researching and re-creating preseventeenth century European history.

The rewards of social and group accomplishment are extensive in this area. Although Mittelstaedt says little about their organizational base, the American Civil War enactments that he writes about are presented throughout the United States, an activity complex and extensive enough to require an association of some kind. The experience of working with others to carry off a dramatic event of these proportions is likely as rewarding as the personal self-actualization and self-enrichment that are also felt. In this activity, both social and personal rewards are impossible to experience without some sort of reenactment organization to bring everyone together.

Turning again to polymorphic organization of leisure, this time of the deviant variety, male heterosexual transvestites, or cross-dressers, meet in local clubs or chapters of a national body known as Society for the Second Self. Local groups exist primarily for display (Feinbloom, 1976, pp. 71–77; Woodhouse, 1989, pp. 23–25). Members typically go to a rented club room or inner-city apartment, where they cross-dress for each other for the sexual thrill this provides, examine samples of feminine apparel and cosmetics, and take pictures of one another dressed as women. Participants in these get-togethers have access to refreshments, soft music, and several wall mirrors. There is also a variety of magazines (fashion and pornographic) and sex-oriented books as well as a notice board filled with announcements. On a typical evening, between five and twenty transvestites are present, most having arrived dressed in women's clothing or having changed into them on the premises. Conversation centers chiefly on sports, work, jokes, and transvestite subjects. A certain amount of picture taking and viewing also occurs. Everyone is expected to refrain from overt displays of sex, such as masturbation. Depending on the participant's level of skill in and knowledge about cross-dressing, it can be classified as either deviant casual leisure of the sensory stimulation type, or deviant hobbyist activity of the activity participation type.

Self-Help Groups

Self-help groups are composed of members sharing a common condition, situations, heritage, symptom, or experience (Lieberman, Borman & associates, 1979, p. 2). They are largely self-governing, self-regulating, and self-supporting; emphasize self-reliance; and generally offer a face-to-face or phone-to-phone contact network that is accessible without charge. Romeder (1990, p. 33) adds that self-help groups may promote personal change, social change, or both.

Katz and Bender (1990, p. 27) have identified five types of self-help groups. One is primarily therapeutic; these groups assistant members with difficult life transitions (e.g., divorce, retirement), pathological conditions (e.g., mental disorder, eating disorders), and stressful situations (e.g., death, rape). Another type is founded on certain principles of advocacy or action; they hope to change existing institutions, policies, services, and the like. For example, they militate against drunk driving or discrimination against the elderly, or argue for new laws for equitable taxation ethnic education. Some self-help groups promote alternative lifestyles, such as those centered on gay liberation or urban residential communes. A fourth type serves people trying to save themselves from mental or physical decline caused by abusive spouses, excessive drink, or compulsive gambling. The fifth type refers to self-help group that combine two or more of the other types as food banks and self-housing programs do.

Most self-help groups appear to be of the grassroots association variety, although there are undoubtedly some that can be classified as informal small groups. The latter exist, if for no other reason, than as the preliminary stage of a future association, whereas their very nature seems to discourage growth leading to the more complex structure of a volunteer organization. The polymorphic structures of, for example, Alcoholics and Gamblers Anonymous are nonetheless exceptions to this generalization; they have paid personnel in their national offices (e.g., secretaries, directors), while unpaid members of the organization effect its therapeutic goals locally.

What is the nature of participation at the local level for members of self-help groups? They are involved there during free time, but are they engaged in a leisure activity? Despite the strong obligation these people typically feel to help their own kind deal with their unfortunate condition, my limited observations in this area suggest that they are pursuing a form of leisure (although I know of no research on this question). First, obligation can be felt in leisure, a condition not necessarily incompatible with the principle that people have a certain amount of freedom (i.e., a freedom always framed in certain constraints) to choose their activities there (Stebbins, 2000b). Second, the leisure pursued in self-help groups appears to be for the most part casual, primarily of the sociable conversational variety. Members who have lived with the condition and adjusted to it (e.g., blindness, multiple sclerosis), or when possible, have overcome it (e.g., drug addiction, mental disorder) talk with members still struggling to adjust. Talk is typically warm and sympathetic, an enjoyable leisure experience for the first but not for the second. The second, who must also be considered members of the group, are too instrumentally oriented to be regarded as partaking of leisure. Their condition forces such participation, much as a toothache forces its sufferer to see a dentist. Therapeutic talk may bring relief, but it would be difficult to qualify this process as leisure activity.

This section has been regrettably speculative, caused in good part by a dearth of research on the leisure character of participation in self-help groups. Thus there is some important scientific work to be done here, in addition to the therapeutic work for which self-help groups are so well-known.

Conclusions

Grassroots associations are ubiquitous in contemporary society and enormously important as vehicles for citizen participation in communal life. The tendency in leisure studies and allied disciplines, particularly psychology and sociology, to study individual motivation to the exclusion of its organizational counterpart has resulted in a paucity of exploratory field data on this question relative to these important collectivities. Since they are highly diverse, it cannot be presumed each will show the same organizational features of motivation, which makes it all the more necessary to examine closely a broad range of organizations.

The problem, in part, is that they are unobtrusive, much like the leisure activities they organize; to the extent that serious leisure is marginal (Stebbins, 2001a, pp. 16–18), so too are the groups in which it is pursued. Out of sight, out of mind, so to speak. Little groups of amateur painters, hobbyist dressmakers, and volunteer tax advisors pale in insignificance in face of their professional and commercial equivalents and their organizations. Still, as long as the first can partake of their chosen leisure with reasonable effectiveness, they are generally disinclined to call attention to themselves. Visibility is not their main goal; rather it is to pursue and experience their free-time activities of choice. As a result, they often get overlooked by social scientists and the larger society alike.

Not so, however, with volunteer and leisure service organizations.

Chapter Four

Volunteer and Leisure Service Organizations

The organizations covered in this chapter are what common sense holds to be proper organizations. True sociological theory allows for a much broader interpretation of organization, which has helped underscore the fact that it is an extremely broad feature of contemporary social life in general and leisure life in particular. Organization is a much broader concept than the formal organizations examined in this chapter. Common sense does not regard dyads and triads as organizations—however correct and enlightening in sociological terms this classification is—while grassroots associations seem more likely to be looked at as clubs or informal groups than real organizations. The crucial distinction separating these sociological organizations from the volunteer and leisure service organizations in this chapter lies in the mix of their formal, large-scale structure.

Formal Large-Scale Organizations

A formal, large-scale organization is a massive social group formed to reach one or more specified goals, for instance, when done during leisure to promote a cause or organize an activity. People comprising the group, for the most part, carry out assigned tasks and routines. They are governed by rules, and everyone in the group has a role to play. The roles and those who fill them are arranged in some sort of hierarchy. Responsibilities within the organization are attached to the role (e.g., position, office), not an individual.

In formal groups, some of which can be small-scale (i.e., small groups, small grassroots associations), rules, roles, and goals are more or less explicit. Like other types of groups, the formal, large-scale organization is held together, in part, by members' recognition of their group as a body of accepted individuals to the exclusion of nonmembers. Moreover, this form of organization, again like some small groups, requires a legal charter. In many countries, volunteer and leisure service organizations also require governmental recognition as nonprofit entities. Finally, compared with many small groups, large-scale organizations tend to have clearly identifiable boundaries established by such formal signs of membership as dues, cards, and pins.

As for size, it has already been observed that, at least in theory, a small group is any organized unit of two to twenty individuals, and that all larger collectivities are considered large-scale organizations. This classification is widely regarded as arbitrary however, for whatever its numerical size, a group becomes "large" when it has so many people that regular interaction is substantially limited and intimacy is no longer experienced—a group becomes large when amount and quality of intermember communication are diluted. Under these conditions more formal arrangements seem unavoidable. Groups with a growing membership and scale of operations are usually forced to become more formal and more complex (i.e., large-scale), if for no other reason than to ensure efficiency of communication and coordination of functions.

Consequently, the matters of formality and complexity of a group may be regarded as falling along a continuum where group structure and operations can be described as informal (least complex), semiformal, or formal (most complex). There is not, then, a clear line separating the groups considered in this chapter from a number of those considered in preceding chapters. Nevertheless, volunteer and leisure service organizations do have their distinctive properties.

Volunteer and Leisure Services Organizations

In Chapter 3 it was stated that both grassroots associations and volunteer organizations fall under the heading of voluntary groups. Smith (2000, p. ix) defined the latter as "nonprofit groups of any type, whether grassroots associations or based on paid staff, and whether local, national, or international in scope." Volunteer organizations are distinguished by their reliance on paid staff, and by the fact that they are established to facilitate work for a cause or provision of a service rather than pursuit of a pastime. They nonetheless depend significantly on volunteer help to reach their goals.

Pearce (1993, p. 15) holds that by far the largest number of volunteers work in these organizations. Some volunteer organizations may be staffed entirely by remunerated employees, with volunteers only being involved as unpaid members of their boards of directors. Hospitals and universities are two main examples. Many foundations can be similarly classified. Other volunteer organizations have a more even mix of paid and volunteer personnel; they include Greenpeace, Amnesty International, and the Red Cross. Finally, some have only one or two employees with all other work being conducted by volunteers. They are, at bottom, grassroots associations that have grown complicated enough to justify hiring someone to help with certain routine operations of the group.

Leisure service organizations are not voluntary groups as just defined. Rather, they are collectivities consisting of a paid staff which provides one or more leisure services to a certain clientele. To be sure, these clients are engaging in particular leisure activities, but the organizations providing them are not themselves leisure organizations of the sort considered in this book. Leisure service organizations are established to either make a profit, the goal of many a health spa, amusement park, and bowling center, for example. In some instances, their goal is simply to make enough money to continue offering their services. This is the goal of charitable, nonprofit groups like Meals-On-Wheels, the YMCA and YWCA, and Elderhostel programs.

What makes leisure service organizations important from a leisure participation standpoint is that they can influence a client's desire to spend some free time in one or more of them. For instance, they can efficiently or inefficiently provide the desired service, provide or fail to provide an atmosphere conducive to social interaction with other clients, and encourage or discourage identification with the organization. Leisure services organizations can make themselves known through aggressive advertising or fail to attract clients because publicity is lacking. They can exclude many clients with high prices or ask a lower price that brings in greater numbers. Leisure service organizations are therefore not to be overlooked. As Godbey (1999, p. 349) observes: "Many of the leisure activities in which you participate are sponsored by a formal organization....formal organizations play an important part in shaping our leisure behavior."

Research on Volunteer Organizations

Volunteer organizations, as the term indicates, offer a leisure outlet for volunteers, some of it casual, some of it the career variety. There are organizations like religious establishments, seniors centers, and political parties that engage copious numbers of both types, in contrast to other organizations like hospitals, primary schools, and the Peace Corps that rely almost exclusively on career volunteers. Finally, some volunteer organizations need, for the most part, only casual help. These include community food banks, the Salvation Army, and groups whose mission is to provide transportation for the elderly. Amateurs and hobbyists rarely, if ever, form volunteer organizations, although polymorphic structures in these two types of leisure commonly include volunteer organizations at the national or international level. They set guidelines and offer important services for constituent grassroots associations functioning locally.

Jone Pearce carried out a landmark exploratory study on the behavior of volunteer workers in Britain, an area of organizational life she says sorely lacks research:

> We know very little about how and why individuals volunteer to work in organizations, and we know even less about how their efforts are organized and directed once they are at work. (1993, p. 3)

She gathered qualitative and quantitative data comparing seven paid-staff with seven volunteer-staff organizations operating across the following range of enterprises: daycare centers, newspaper publishers, poverty relief agencies and symphonic orchestras as well as gift shops, fire departments, and family planning clinics. Volunteers in these organizations worked as musicians, reporters, daycare providers, sales personnel, and the like.

Pearce (1993) found that feelings of personal importance to the organization and extensive social involvement with its members (both paid staff and other volunteers) were rewards of sufficient appeal to generate substantial commitment to the organization. There were also costs, however; some poignant enough to drive a number of volunteers from their organizations. One such cost was the extensive uncertainty about who is a volunteer as well as about the nature of tasks, performance, and role expectations. Lack of recognition of useful skills that some volunteers bring to the organization was a further complaint. Also low levels of congeniality were occasionally mentioned as a problem (Pearce, 1993, p. 55).

Experiencing the costs and rewards of volunteering in these groups was also related to a volunteer's status as core or peripheral member. Core volunteers (also called key volunteers) assume significant levels of responsibility for running the organization's volunteer operations, while peripheral volunteers are less active. Peripheral volunteers follow directives emanating from the core, many having to do with coordination of volunteer activities. Pearce also found that, compared with their core counterparts, peripheral members spent less time working for the organization and contributed less to its operations. One cost of being a core member is continually having to train new volunteers, because previously trained volunteers have left in response to feelings that, for them, the costs and rewards had reached an unfavorable balance (Pearce, 1993, pp. 56–57). As for core members, this situation creates excessive work, a condition that severely tests their own commitment, while raising the spectre that they might burnout.

A well-known cost in the world of organizational volunteering is the conflict that occasionally flares up between volunteer boards of directors and paid staff. Amis, Slack, and Berrett (1995) examined this tension in four sports organizations in Canada. The authors learned that these conflicts amount to far more than mere interpersonal differences. Rather, they stem from the ways in which units of a particular organization are differentiated and the degree to which these units are interdependent. This is exemplified in one of their case studies of a small non-Olympic sports organization:

> A number of members and former members of the Board, however, felt that the problems within the organization were more the fault of the ED [executive director]. Upon joining the organization, as the lone employee, the ED assumed responsibility for every office function. As the organization grew in size, and more staff were hired, the Board expected the ED's role to evolve into one of an office manager. It was this perceived change in role which caused many of the problems in the organization, according to one director. The director realized that the organization was "losing a lot of [their] top quality [staff] to other sports." He questioned a number of the office staff to ascertain why there was such a high turnover of personnel, and why the office was so slow in producing reports. The staff responded that although they were given responsibility to carry out a variety of tasks, they were never actually provided with the authority to perform them. (Amis, Slack & Berrett, 1995, pp. 9–10)

Amis and his colleagues concluded that the voluntary character of these sport organizations magnifies significantly the possibility of conflict. Members of an organization's board of directors and its operational core number among "key volunteers" (Stebbins, 1998b, pp. 4–5). These volunteers are highly committed community servants working in one, sometimes two or three, official and responsible posts within one or more established grassroots associations or volunteer organizations. President, vice-president, treasurer, and secretary were the most common posts in the grassroots associations and volunteer organizations in the minority francophone communities of Calgary and Edmonton. Additionally, chairing an important committee or directing a major program, for example, were also found to contribute greatly to the maintenance and development of those communities. None of these positions is remunerated, although, in increasingly rare circumstances, a president or director may receive a minor honorarium. The organizations and most of the associations, which in these communities are typically small, are legally chartered. The associations that are not are nonetheless well-established, having existed long enough to have become highly visible locally. Indeed, for some clubs and friendship groups, it is unnecessary to be formally constituted. As for volunteer organizations, it is rare to have more than one paid employee.

Key volunteers are distinguished from other types of volunteers by at least four criteria. First, presidents, treasurers, and the like have complex, extensive responsibilities whose execution affects the functioning of their association or organization in important ways. Second, such positions are enduring. Officers are usually elected for a year, and chairs and directors may serve even longer. Third, success of associations and organizations in which key volunteers serve contributes significantly to maintenance and development of the local community of like-minded people (e.g., same ethnic group, leisure interest, environmental stance, self-help concern). Fourth, key volunteers have a high degree of commitment both to their collectivities and through them to these two community goals as this study clearly shows. These criteria square with Van Til's and Smith's definitions of volunteering and voluntary altruism.

At first glance, activity of this kind might look more like work without pay than anything else. In fact, a number of respondents in this study defined their own key volunteering precisely in these terms. Nevertheless, after examining their definitions, Stebbins (2000c) concluded that by and large their volunteering is a special kind of leisure—a form of career volunteering.

This study of key volunteers in these two urban francophone communities is the only one to directly consider within the framework of leisure

theory the question of how leisure organizations motivate people to participate in them to date. Of the ten rewards of serious leisure, four stood out
as especially salient for the volunteers interviewed in this study. Two of
these were personal—self-enrichment and self-enhancement—which are
related to the self-interestedness question raised earlier. The other two—
group accomplishment and contribution to maintenance and development
of the local francophone community—were, however, more social and altruistic. Being a member of, for example, a francophone theater company, community and cultural centre, or organization representing all French-speaking
people in the area, and especially being a key volunteer there, is powerfully
attractive. Why? Because it gives the member an opportunity to lead the
group toward particular goals and, by way of such group accomplishment,
help maintain and further develop the larger minority community.

Yet, there were costs as well. The francophone study, the only research
so far to examine costs in career volunteering, revealed a variety of tensions
and dislikes, although no significant disappointments. According to the
study, many tensions have to do in one way or another with the volunteer's
family life, which when school-age children are present, can be especially
problematic. One tension—the *temporal tension*—centers on the need for
constant planning and scheduling, two principal ways of making the most
efficient use of scarce time. Temporal tensions were felt mostly during the
workweek, since respondents with children tended to avoid volunteering on
weekends where daytime hours were reserved for family-related activities
and domestic obligations.

Furthermore, *relational tension* can occur. This is the friction that sometimes boils up between spouse and volunteer, or children and volunteer when
a volunteer engagement is chosen over demands of the other. Respondents
experiencing this tension uniformly qualified it as a main cost of volunteering, and through constant planning, tried their utmost to avoid it, pro-
claiming in face of occasional failure that, nevertheless, "Family comes
first over volunteering."

Obligative tension is the stress arising from inability to meet various
domestic requirements in the face of volunteer commitments of higher
priority. Several respondents mentioned feeling guilty for failing to perform
certain repair, maintenance, and housekeeping duties. This tension can
also be relational when failure to do a chore or do it satisfactorily irritates
another member of the family.

An especially thorny variant of obligative tension revolves around
the question of who prepares evening meals when both parents volunteer
at that time. To make matters worse, solving this tension tends to beget

another temporal tension, since responsibility for a particular weekday dinner must be set well in advance for the parent at home that afternoon and evening. When both parents have to be away from home the same evening, their children, if young, become the focus of a special obligative tension. That is, they must hire a babysitter (additional advanced planning), a necessity made more complicated in linguistically endogamous households where this person must meet not only the usual moral standards for this responsibility but also the language requirement of speaking passable French in this case. Such people can be difficult to find in Canada's dominantly anglophone cities, and when found, may live at some distance from the volunteer's home.

Finally, some respondents experienced *leisure tension,* which unlike the preceding tensions, is mainly positive. That is, committed to certain volunteer roles (leisure), they then discovered how little time they had for other leisure activities they were also fond of. The volunteers in this study nearly always resolved this tension by favoring volunteering, though often not without the disquieting recognition that they were missing something interesting and satisfying. On this note, a handful of respondents said they had no leisure, or more accurately, no *other* leisure.

Schedule conflicts among volunteer commitments constituted an especially annoying variant of the leisure tension for several interviewees. Missing, for example, a meeting of the board of directors of the theater society, of which one is secretary, to attend a meeting of the parish council, of which one is chair, would be most bothersome for these interviewees. This person would be annoyed, in part, because it is known that effective coordination of community volunteer activities is possible.

When respondents in this study were asked to discuss their dislikes apropos of their pursuits, I indicated my interest lay in more serious matters than pet peeves. Dislikes are problems requiring volunteers to adjust significantly, possibly even to leave the volunteer role. It turned out that, in these two francophone communities, as most everywhere else in life, annoyances were commonplace, whereas deeper dislikes were much rarer. On the one hand, all but three respondents could describe at least one substantially disagreeable aspect of key volunteering. On the other hand, very few could describe more than two.

The two most prominent dislikes were organizational; they were the behavior of *difficult persons* and the shortage of *reliable volunteers.* Difficult persons are infamous for their propensity to complain excessively about all sorts of issues while being exceptionally critical of others. Fortunately, such people are uncommon in these two communities, though when present, they are consequently more conspicuous. The problem of too few reliable volunteers baffled leaders in both cities, since many francophones who could serve as volunteers live there.

Types of Leisure Service Organizations

Godbey (1999, pp. 353–357) discusses several types of leisure service organizations. The *neutral provider* attempts to identify and supply leisure experiences in which certain groups of people want to participate. Municipal parks and recreation departments operate at times in this capacity. Other service organizations serve as *change agents,* providing activities their directors believe people should be involved in (e.g., company fitness programs, after-school programs for youth). Some leisure service organizations function as *coordinators of leisure opportunities.* Schools and municipal park and recreation departments also do this, as do YMCAs and YWCAs. Additionally, organizations are established to provide leisure for the *recreationally dependent,* such as people who are poor or have handicaps. Most of the organizations listed in this paragraph operate on a nonprofit basis.

Other organizations—the most pervasive in the leisure service field (Godbey, 1999, p. 361)—are for-profit establishments. One type promotes *specific leisure activities and facilities,* such as bowling centers, skating arenas, golf courses, and bingo halls. Services that *enhance the physical environment* work to provide good boating, fishing, hunting, or camping experiences. Related to the change agents are the *health promoters;* they organize activities for people who yearn to improve their health and conditioning. Of course, their clients need no persuading in this regard, just an opportunity to pursue this kind of leisure, whereas the clients of change agents have to be encouraged to take up the leisure being offered. Some organizations—among them Elderhostel and programs in continuing education—provide *leisure education,* offering this service across a great range of amateur and hobbyist activities. Finally, *promoters and facilitators of tourism* deal in one of the most sought after forms of leisure in the twenty-first century.

Examples of Leisure Service

The gyms at which bodybuilders shape up are a form of leisure service organization, and they have attracted scholarly attention on how they influence participation there. Most accurately classified as a health promoter or promoter of specific leisure, if not both, the gym is a business where the clients are mainly amateur weightlifters. In some instances, they work out alongside a small number of professionals whose livelihood rests on contest earnings and endorsements. Klein (1986) likened the American gym he studied to a feudal structure composed in descending order of the following ranks: owners, professional bodybuilders, amateur bodybuilders, gym rats (noncompetitors), members at large (train less than the others), onlookers, and pilgrims. Onlookers go to gyms to satisfy their curiosity about what goes on inside them, while pilgrims go there to "pay homage to the place" (Klein, 1986, p. 121). Within each rank, or strata, individuals compete with each other for recognition of best physique and, to the extent applicable, for acquisition of economic opportunities (e.g., remunerative contests and endorsements).

To be at or near the top of this structure is itself an incentive, which however, can only be realized at a gym, the leisure organization within which this structure evolves. Likewise, the gym fosters at each rank numerous dyadic relationships between mentors and subordinates, through which the second aspire to mount the hierarchy guided by tutelage from the first. Still, whereas gyms do provide some organizational reasons for pursuing bodybuilding as leisure, and for some, as work, this activity, Klein concludes, is highly individualistic. It is motivated by, among other hopes, those of becoming more physically attractive and healthier of mind and body as well as meeting the ideals of heterosexuality.

Senior centers exemplify the recreationally dependent type of leisure service provider. Cutler and Danigelis (1993, p. 159) conclude, following a review of the sparse literature on this subject, that results of research on how these establishments affect the well-being of people who use them are inconsistent. One study found no relationship whatsoever between life satisfaction and participation in senior centers, whereas another showed participants to be less depressed than nonparticipants. A third study found that current users of these centers have higher levels of life satisfaction than former users. Unfortunately, methodological weaknesses dog research in this area, preventing any firm conclusions at this time about the motivational properties of senior centers for their users.

Butsch (1984), in his study of commodification of the model airplane hobby in the United States, sheds some light on the neutral provider type of leisure service provision. We are not concerned here, however, with the companies that as far back as the 1930s sold kits, supplies, and information for building model airplanes. Hobbyists in this field were only clients of these establishments, even if a few of the former actually founded some of these firms. But then, as now, many of these hobbyists belonged to the Academy of Model Aeronautics (AMA), which since 1936 has run national meets as well as established and disseminated rules and regulations for its network of local clubs and AMA-licensed local contests.

For model airplane hobbyists the motivational component in this arrangement is simple: competing in AMA contests requires membership in this organization. Although Butsch never discussed this aspect of the model airplane pastime, it is probably also true that local AMA clubs are sources of good friendships, important technical information, and nearly endless talk about the hobby. The national body also publishes a magazine and national newsletter. Still, this is a polymorphic form of leisure organization, with both levels offering something important for members of the AMA. For instance, its leadership, presumably on advice from the rank-and-file, let the companies know that the AMA was unhappy with their failure to do their share in supporting aeromodeling and the Academy. Through the national AMA, then, members can exercise some control over some of the forces affecting them.

There are, to my knowledge, no studies of motivation to participate in leisure education as provided by a leisure service organization. Nonetheless, various general observations have been made, which sketch some of the motivational links between individual participants and, say, a community adult education program. For example, Selman, Cooke, Selman, and Dampier (1998, pp. 29–30) list four functions of adult education as seen through the eyes of individual participants in it, three of which—the social (roles in community), recreational, and self-developmental functions—bear directly on leisure. That is, by way of learning and in harmony with these functions, the authors see adult education as contributing to the maintenance and development of the individual or the society, if not both. This, then, is "liberal adult education" (Duke, 1994).

But what types of leisure constitute the true focus of liberal adult education? It has been argued here that leisure is not all of a kind. In other words, people hardly need a course to learn how to take an afternoon nap, stroll in the park, or gorge themselves on beer and pretzels, activity defined earlier as casual leisure. Hence, the leisure learned through adult education is usually of the serious variety (Stebbins, 2001a, p. 95), with casual leisure courses constituting rare exceptions (e.g., courses on how to relax or be a good conversationalist).

This having been said, adult education organizations even fail to serve all serious leisure interests (Stebbins, 2001a, pp. 96–97). Amateurs in the arts and sciences can avail themselves of adult education courses and in the arts, even programs that further their learning of serious leisure pursuits. The same holds for most individual amateur sports (e.g., golf, tennis, racquetball). Still, if we examine the totality of adult educational programs in the typical North American city, it is clear these organizations ignore some amateur activities. Thus, would-be participants in such sports as handball, rodeo, weightlifting, and auto and motorcycle racing must usually learn on their own, using books, watching others play, and asking countless questions. Moreover, virtually all entertainment arts skills must be acquired this way.

Humber College in Toronto has developed an adult education course on stand-up comedy. The one-week "workshop" was offered for the first time in 1997 (Clark, 1997). There may also be isolated adult education courses of this sort on juggling, ventriloquism, and entertainment magic, for example, even though the general rule is that learning these arts is mainly self-directed; that is, usually accomplished by reading, watching, questioning, and in some instances, arranging for private tutoring.

Adult education is, except for collecting, a main avenue for learning hobbies. A great range of making and tinkering activities fills the multitude of North American adult education catalogs. They include baking, decorating, do-it-yourself, raising and breeding, and various crafts. The same is true for activity participation, which encompasses such diverse passions as skin diving, cross-country skiing, mushroom gathering, and ballroom dancing. Here, too, activities exist whose enthusiasts usually have no choice but to learn on their own, among them hiking, fishing (except fly casting), snowmobiling, barbershop singing, and dirt (trail) bike riding. Moreover, adult education courses are rare for the many would-be players of hobbyist sports or games (i.e., those falling outside the category of amateur-professional sport). Most people in this area must direct their own learning of darts, horseshoes, handball, or table tennis, to name a few. Those who play a particular table, board, card, or electronic game usually learned it from other players or printed instructions, sometimes from both. Still, adult education courses are readily available on bridge, orienteering, and martial arts. Finally, the liberal arts hobbies are most often developed purely through self-direction, chiefly by reading, as noted earlier. Again we find exceptions, as in the general interest courses on certain arts, cultures, philosophies, and histories. Moreover, language instruction—a liberal art—is one of the pillars of adult education.

Adult education courses related to volunteerism center mostly in such areas as fundraising, management, and recruitment of volunteers. To the extent that serious leisure volunteers are involved in these areas, they are likely to be interested in courses about them. Many career volunteers devote themselves to other tasks, which they learn about outside the framework of adult education. That is, the grassroots association or volunteer organization in which they are serving provides the basic instruction they need to have while on the job. For this reason volunteers fall beyond the scope of this section.

Commercial provision of specific leisure activities and facilities is pervasive in modern society. Yet at times in this sphere, the link between provider as organization and client as consumer of its leisure is far more tenuous than previously described, making it difficult to identify motivational relationships between the two. Movie houses, television stations, and amusement parks, for example, provide specific leisure activities, but the most that can be said about them in motivational terms is that clients find diversion attractive there. Direct interaction with employees of the organization providing the diversion is, at most, minimal. Consequently, these organizations lack the capacity to, for instance, organize a hierarchical system as the bodybuilding gym does, develop instructor–student relationships as the adult education course does, or serve as pressure group for change as the model airplane association does. Much of the provision of casual leisure in today's world is of this nature, which to the extent would-be participants are aware of other forms of organized leisure, helps explain their appeal for them.

This is not true, however, for promoters and facilitators of tourism, who form clear, sometimes involved relationships with their clients. Thus travel agents, although they may talk over the telephone, nevertheless discuss with individual clients their travel needs. Such talk, especially if the planned trip is long and complicated, can be extensive and occasionally personal (e.g., family budget limits, taste in hotels and restaurants, feelings about foreign cultures).

Once the holiday is underway other relationships may develop depending on how adventuresome the traveler. Yiannakis and Gibson (1992, p. 291), in a synthetic classification of types of tourists, identified fourteen, of which three—the "anthropologist," "archaeologist," and "explorer"—bear on this condition. Anthropologists and archaeologists take arranged tours, the first because they enjoy meeting local people, trying their food, and speaking their language, the second because they enjoy viewing archaeological sites and ruins as part of their historical study of ancient civilizations. In both instances, they establish a relationship with their guide and possibly other people who help make the tour possible. Explorers have interests similar to those of anthropologists, but pursue them through trips arranged on their own. Though they might use the services of a travel agent to get to and from their holiday destination, once there they, for the most part, have little further to do with the tourism business as leisure provider.

People who travel to resorts for sun, surf, gambling, and relaxation but never leave the premises for even a guided tour have, for the most part, a relationship with leisure providers only slightly more personal than that described earlier for movie houses, television stations, and the like. Checking into a hotel, buying drinks and meals, renting a cabana on the beach, and so on are typically fleeting, superficial transactions. Relations with croupiers and card dealers in the casino might be slightly more profound and enduring, but in most instances not significantly so. In short, for these vacationers, their deepest contact with promoters and facilitators of tourism occurs back home during the planning stage of their holiday.

Conclusions

Because they serve clients rather than recruit and direct volunteers and other types of leisure participants, leisure service organizations escape (at the client level) the burnout problem that sometimes plagues volunteer organizations. Glogow (1986) says burnout among volunteers can appear in up to three ways: loss of concern for people with whom one is working, emotional exhaustion, and exhaustion from excessive demands on energy. Gabard (1997) found in a study of AIDS service organizations in California that the two most important reasons their volunteers gave for quitting them were much like reasons such people give for quitting other volunteer organizations. One, a greater priority than serving in the AIDS organization comes up. Two, problems develop with the administrative or organizational structure of the group.

Signs and symptoms of burnout constituted only a distant third reason for leaving the AIDS group. Moreover, this burnout had less to do with client contact than with disagreeable matters like long hours, paperwork, insufficient training, bureaucratic hassles, and so on. Gabard concludes that, since volunteers have much greater opportunity to avoid burnout than paid staff, we should expect it not to be a leading cause of attrition. The former, by dint of the fact that they are pursuing a form of leisure, have more control over their involvement than the latter. Therefore they can quit before or at the point where volunteering shows signs of burning them out.

The much publicized condition of burnout appears to be more problematic for people at work than for those at leisure. Although conceivable that burnout could strike a person intently pursuing any form of serious leisure in one of the organizations considered so far, not just someone volunteering in volunteer organizations, this appears unlikely. Unlikely, because participants have considerable control over their involvement in this area of life. This is especially true for leisure sought in the post-traditional tribe.

Chapter Five
Tribes

To this point, most readers will have been familiar with the organizations considered along the way. Two- and three-person relationships, small groups, social networks, grassroots associations, and volunteer and leisure services organizations are important, omnipresent features of everyday life. To be sure, the nonspecialist cannot usually classify and conceptualize these so neatly as was done here, and often identifies them by other terms, albeit at times inaccurately from a scientific point of view. Not so, however, with the organizations considered in this chapter and the next: tribes and social worlds. Even though legitimate organizations according to the definition set out in Chapter 1, these lack the common sense appearance of being such, and perhaps for this reason, most people are simply unaware that they exist. Still, many an enthusiast participates in them, subtly charmed in significant measure by none other than their attractive organizational properties.

The Global, Postmodern Tribe

While it is true that among certain primitive peoples, tribes function as an important form of local social organization, these kinship groups are really only a metaphor for Michel Maffesoli (1996). Instead, he transforms this narrow anthropological concept into a much broader, sociological one that identifies and describes a postmodern phenomenon spanning national borders. In this regard, he observes that mass culture has disintegrated, leaving in its wake a diversity of "tribes." These tribes are fragmented groupings left over from the preceding era of mass consumption, groupings recognized today by their unique tastes, lifestyles, and form of social organization.

These groupings exist for the pleasure of their members to share the warmth of being together, socializing with each other, seeing and touching each other, and so on—a highly emotional process. In this they are both participants and observers, as exemplified by in-group hairstyles, bodily modifications, and items of apparel. This produces a sort of solidarity among members not unlike that found in the different religions and primitive tribes. Moreover, being together under these conditions can lead to a kind of spontaneous creativity that gives rise to widely varied, new cultural forms having appeal for great masses of people. Not all these new forms are negative or deviant, even though it is clear that some spawn local racism and ostracism (e.g., skinheads). Nevertheless, they do beget distinctive "lifestyles," although much less complicated ones than those springing from serious leisure pursuits. The postmodern world is, among other things, a "multiplicity of lifestyles—a kind of multiculturalism."

Maffesoli argues further that today's tribes serve as antidotes to the dominant individualism of our time, for individual identity is submerged in such groups. They are not, however, without ideals. Rather he observes that "it would perhaps be better to note that [tribes] have no vision of what should constitute the absolutes of a society. Each group has its own absolute" (Maffesoli, 1996, pp. 88–89). There is, moreover, a secret sharing among members of the emotions and experiences unique to their tribe, which reinforces close group ties and distinguishes insiders from outsiders. As for context, postmodern tribalism must be seen as a product of the massified metropolis—a distinctively urban phenomenon.

Much of postmodern tribalization has taken place in the sphere of leisure, where it has given birth to a small number of interest-based, serious leisure tribes and a considerably larger number of taste-based, casual leisure tribes. Although Maffesoli (1996) fails to recognize these two leisure forms, Rob Shields briefly mentions them his foreword to the English translation of the former's book:

> Typical examples of *tribus* [tribes] are not only fashion victims, or youth subcultures. This term can be extended to interest-based collectivities: hobbyists; sports enthusiasts; and more important, environmental movements, user-groups of state services, and consumer lobbies. (1996, p. xi)

In addition, although there is no gainsaying that serious leisure and its enthusiasts are marginal in ways set out earlier in this book, this condition in postmodern times seems only to enhance their sense of tribal (i.e., organizational) belonging. When the larger community sees these tribes as quaint, eccentric, or simply different, solidarity among members is strengthened to a significant degree, even though all must live with this unfavorable image. Meanwhile, in some forms of tribal serious leisure, a small number of leisure organizations provide their members with socially visible rallying points for individualized leisure identities as well as outlets for the central life interest they share. Most often this organization is a club, which nevertheless serves as an important axis for the lifestyle enjoyed by enthusiasts pursuing the associated serious leisure activity.

The casual leisure tribes are unable to offer this more complex level of organizational belonging, in that they rarely, if ever, become even this formally organized. These tribes retain too much of their former character as consumer masses to serve as the seedbed for formal groups and organizations as considered in preceding chapters. There is, of course, a true sense of belonging that comes with sharing private symbols with other members of the same mass (Maffesoli, 1996, pp. 76–77, 96–100). Yet, the feeling of solidarity that comes with belonging to, for example, a small group or grassroots association is commonly missing in taste-based tribes.

Taste-based tribes are especially popular among contemporary youth, being a main trend these days in this age category and favored over earlier tendencies to join established groups. Roberts, in writing about their tribes, observes that

> the groups of young people (and adults) who become players in, or fans of spectator sports teams, and who attend "raves" and similar scenes where their drugs of choice are available and their preferred types of music are played, can experience intense camaraderie…. Much of the appeal of these occasions is that they are incredibly social. Individuals find that they are accepted and experience a sense of belonging. None of this is completely new. The change over time has been that the young people who play together nowadays have rarely grown up together and attended the same local schools. Their sole bond is likely to be leisure taste or activity. Yet being part of these scenes can be extremely important to those involved. (1997, p. 9)

Taste-based tribes, however, as the next section clearly shows, are not the exclusive social domain of young people.

Taste-Based Tribes

Taste-based tribes organize a very large number of individuals (thousands, even millions of them) who share a common appreciation for a certain activity or item of popular culture. This darling of the collective eye can be, for instance, a style of art, music, or clothing; a form of dance or amusement, or even a make of automobile or tape player. Whatever it is, its raison d'être is basically hedonic: it organizes a type of casual leisure that attracts and holds members of the tribe primarily through sociable conversation, sensory stimulation, passive or active entertainment, or a combination of these.

To my knowledge no one has surveyed and classified the world's tribes, leaving us without proper estimate of their extent and prevalence. One reason for this is that direct scientific recognition of the phenomenon dates only to Maffesoli's recent work. Nonetheless, a handful of studies of tribes have been carried out in the past two decades that can be analyzed from the tribal perspective, even while their authors used other frameworks.

Friesen's (1990) study of fans of heavy metal music in Calgary is part of this small corpus. Although not strictly analyzed from the perspective of leisure tribes, it nonetheless clearly shows that these fans help make up one. He found that this music—a genre of rock that got its start in the 1960s—was extremely important to his sample of young people; next to friendship it was their greatest source of personal enjoyment. Moreover, the music was listened to in the company of others who also enjoyed it. In this organizational setting some participants would get drunk, do drugs (chiefly cannabis substances), engage in sex—but above all have a party. Friesen found that an important part of the sense of belonging to their tribe was defending their music to the world beyond it, which tended then, as now, to marginalize both it and its fans as deviant:

> Some adherents to heavy metal are drawn to the music because of its distinctiveness; it helps to give them a feeling of individuality. Soon, they are labeled deviant by dint of their association with the heavy metal subculture. For others the deviant identity is acquired through "hassles" with police and other established groups in society and their attempts to label headbangers as such.
>
> It is not unusual, then, to find headbangers (particularly males) identifying themselves as deviant. (Friesen, 1990, p. 73)

Heavy metal underwent its most recent of several revivals in the latter half of the 1990s. Therefore it still numbers among the many contemporary tribes.

The rave scene, like that of heavy metal, is also an international tribe. It is possible that this form has received more research attention than any of the others. Here young people in many parts of the world gather together from time to time in all-night sessions held in a warehouse, private club, or even a remote field or barn to dance and listen to their choice of DJ-provided music. Use of such drugs as LSD, cannabis, ecstasy, and amphetamines is not uncommon at these gatherings, which are graced with such special effects as dramatic videos and variegated moving lights. Locating the venue some distance from "civilization" has been a way for sponsors of the rave to keep costs under control.

Critcher (2000) notes that by 1993 in Britain "rave" as a term was heard with decreasing frequency and use of ecstacy had passed its peak. The rave and its successors had become incorporated into the inner-city club industry there. Nonetheless, the phenomenon continues in Britain as well as elsewhere. Weber (1999) observed that the raves he studied in Toronto were attractive to participants because they offered an interesting venue, an occasion to be with friends, and an opportunity to listen and dance to their preferred style of music. People who showed up only to consume drugs were castigated by the sample as misguided, as not attending the rave for the right reasons of enjoyment of friends, music, and the scene.

The tendency today at a particular rave is to feature one style of music (e.g., reggae, Afro-Pop). Preferred styles change rapidly, however—an enduring quality of popular music since its inception. Several web sites list upcoming raves in various cities and regions around the world, thus giving this tribe more organization than many others.

"Trekkies" and "Trekkers" have emerged as names for the highly dedicated viewing audience of the TV series "Star Trek" and related films. Since 1966 when the TV series began, they have evolved into a tribe consisting of, in contrast to the two just considered, young *and* middle-aged adults. To be sure, Trekkies are entertained as they watch installments of "Star Trek," but they also gain considerable satisfaction in identifying and analyzing the many Freudian themes and stereotypic sex roles that characterize each show (Deegan, 1983). For instance, Captain Kirk and his circle of scientific and medical officers symbolize and embody traditional sexual divisions of labor, enact romantic scripts, and seek sex and adventure. Women in the program also have traditional values; they long for love and marriage.

Its comparatively more complex level of organization suggests this tribe might also be analyzed as a liberal arts hobby using the framework of social world (see Chapter 6). Trekkies have their own fanzines, books, newsletters, artifacts, and conventions. An 87-minute documentary film called *Trekkies* was released in 1999, and a home page complete with interactive chat is available on the Internet.

Constituting at least as organizationally complex a tribe as the Trekkies are the dedicated followers of soap operas, also an international pastime (even though these programs tend to differ from one country to the next). Babrow (1990) studied a sample of American university students who routinely watched "soaps." He found that sociality—talk with other students about the program as it is being broadcast—

> is both a vehicle for collectively infusing the shows with meaning and an outcome of the exposure experience. The shows' meaning, both intellectual and emotional, arise as viewers offer histories, interpretations, evaluations, and predictions; meaning also arises as viewers take on roles and bond themselves with other viewers…. The present study suggests that some social viewing contexts are recognized and sought out as pleasant places to simultaneously enjoy soap operas and other audience members (friends, fellow soap opera fans). (p. 349)

Babrow concluded that sociality is actually a motive for watching these programs. He gathered his data in part through participant observation in a student bar where soaps were regularly broadcast on television and in part by questionnaire, with approximately 58% of respondents being female.

Mary Ellen Brown (1994) interviewed several small samples of female soap opera fans in Australia and the United States. Although some women watch them alone, most have some kind of social involvement with other women who like the same programs. Her interviewees were not members of fan clubs, but rather members of networks composed of small numbers of family or friends.

She also noted a second level of fanship, defined as all people who watch a particular soap. Second order people, she explains, meet

> in buses, at work, at school, or somewhere else in passing, find that they watch such-and-such a soap opera, and discuss the current issues on that soap opera with them. Sometimes these people are never seen again, but often they are acquaintances whose major connection is their soap opera friendship. (Brown, 1994, p. 80)

A taste-based tribe to be sure, but one that has been around for decades, predating even television when soaps were available only on radio. This indicates that birth of the postmodern tribe goes much farther back in time than the postmodern epoch about which Maffesoli writes. Maffesoli (1996, p. 95) does note in passing that tribalism is found frequently throughout human history, especially during periods of cultural change.

Beyond the appeal of sociable conversation with family and friends on intriguing happenings in the latest broadcasts of their favorite soap, lies what Brown (1994) calls the "pleasure of resistance." That is, this tribe also offers female members numerous opportunities to resist through talk with one another subtle oppression of the dominant, largely male culture. The cultures of the home and women's concerns are devalued in male culture, which includes a depreciatory estimation of the soap opera itself, in part because the genre has been designed to appeal to women and their stereotyped place in society. Soap opera fan clubs and gossip networks (some of which are now electronic) allow members to create personal meanings as they go about their daily lives, while the soap magazines bring additional grist to this mill. Brown found that, in these meanings, women are almost always dominant and in control, despite the fact that all is fiction.

Activity-Based Tribes

Shields's observation presented earlier in this chapter stating that the concept of tribe can be extended to such interest-based collectivities as hobbyists and sports enthusiasts raises a theoretical question. Can an activity, as opposed to a cultural taste, become the basis for a distinct tribe? This question is answered by determining where the collectivity in question falls on the continuum of structural complexity of organizations, which in this case, runs from the most elementary tribe at the pole of simplest organizations to the most evolved social world at the opposite pole of most complex organizations.

At its simplest a tribe is little more than awareness among a mass of individuals that, in at least some parts of the world, there are people sharing their special taste in music, clothing, bodily adornments, and similar items of popular culture. They therefore feel special attachment and belonging whenever some of them meet face to face. After all, it was noted earlier that tribes are fragmented groupings left over from the days of mass consumption, groupings now known for their unique tastes and lifestyles. Adding newsletters, web sites, and so on increases the complexity of a tribe's organizational structure, pushing it as a type of organization toward the social-world pole of the continuum.

Because serious leisure participants generally pursue their leisure in highly complex organizational settings—including participants identified by Shields as hobbyists and sports enthusiasts (taken here to mean players of sport)—they are best analyzed within the social world perspective (see Chapter 6). They are anything but scions of former mass consumption groupings, and examining them within that framework would profoundly underestimate the complex motivational pull of the social world in which each activity is embedded. Still, all continua dealing with discrete or separable phenomena (as opposed to continuous phenomena like temperature and shades of color) evoke the problem of the cutting point: where does one type end and another begin. Put differently, it is evident that some serious leisure activities fall closer to the tribal pole than others.

The serious leisure activities found closest to the tribal pole are the liberal arts hobbies (see Figure 1). As mentioned, Trekkies and some soap opera fans, because their tribes are reasonably complex, can also be analyzed from this perspective. Are there others? Yes, quite possibly. Although the matter has never been studied through research, it is theoretically possible to separate buffs from consumers in the liberal arts hobbies of sport, cuisine, and the fine and entertainment arts. Some people, call them *consumers*, more or less uncritically consume restaurant fare, sports events, or displays of art (e.g., concerts, shows, exhibitions) as pure entertainment and sensory stimulation (casual leisure), whereas others, call them *buffs*, participate in these same situations as more or less knowledgeable experts, as serious leisure.

	Taste-based Tribes (e.g., music, clothing)	Activity-based Tribes: Consumers (e.g., jazz, basketball)	Activity-based Tribes: Buffs (e.g., Star Trek, opera)	Social Worlds (e.g., amateurs, career volunteers)	
LEAST COMPLEX					→ MOST COMPLEX
	Casual Leisure	Casual Leisure	Serious Leisure	Serious Leisure	

Figure 1   Structural Complexity: From Tribes to Social Worlds

Thus, it is casual leisure when a consumer goes to a French restaurant and does little more than enjoy a good meal. Whereas it is serious leisure when a buff goes and not only enjoys the meal but also reflects on such technical questions as the spices used in the meal, methods of cooking it, presentation on the plate, and sophisticated alternatives to these. This buff-gourmet has the added advantage over the consumer of experiencing some of the rewards that come with participating in any form of serious leisure. The same can be said for people attending symphony concerts, art exhibitions, dance performances, even stand-up comedy shows. Most go as consumers to be entertained, while a smaller (probably much smaller) number go as buffs to be entertained *as well as* to exercise their analytic skills and increase their knowledge of an art they love.

Still, both buffs and consumers fall toward the tribal pole of the organizational structure continuum, although research would likely show that, on the one hand, consumers can be properly categorized as taste-based tribes. Regular consumers of, say, jazz, symphonic music, professional theater, or fine-arts painting often go to shows, concerts, and exhibitions with friends sharing this same taste, and all are aware that certain people elsewhere in the world have acquired similar tastes and that, for this reason, such people are special. Beyond this, however, there is typically little social organization. Avid consumers of professional soccer, hockey, or basketball, among other sports, show similar levels of interest and organization.

Buffs, on the other hand, can be regarded as coalescing into activity-based tribes, even if their leisure world is only somewhat more complicated than that of consumers in the same field. For instance, symphony music buffs can further develop themselves by reading reviews of concerts written by critics known for their acumen in this art. They can also read a vast book-length literature, including several encyclopedias and handbooks, covering the lives of celebrated composers, directors, and performers as well as key historical developments in this field. Taking in some television documentaries, guided tours of famous concert halls and composers' homes, and adult education personal interest courses on this subject, help round out the long list of ways in which symphony music buffs can go well beyond simply consuming the art.

It is likewise for those whose hobby is following jazz, dance, theater, or professional sport. At minimum, one or two periodicals regularly provide information for avid lay enthusiasts in these pursuits (e.g., *Jazz Times*, *Dance Magazine*, *Art in America*, *Sports Illustrated*). Today, every major professional sport usually has some locally televised commentary about teams and players attention focused on weekly performance and seasonal progress. In such fields, by the way, tribal formations are hardly of recent origin, since buffs in these areas have been around for as long as a century or two, depending on the art or sport.

Conclusions

Tribes, especially those based on taste, are commonplace in today's world. Together they give both youth and older generations a wide range of choice of things to do in a collective setting, however abstract it may be at times. Furthermore, people may participate in several tribes and when tired of them, quit, to become involved at their will in one or more others. The result nowadays for many individuals, as Maffesoli (1996, p. 89) observes, is an individualized existence consisting of a multiplicity of lifestyles, of distinctive shared patterns of behavior organized around one or a handful of powerful interests. The central interest is the activity or cultural item sought, a style of music, clothing, hairdo, and the various social practices associated with it. Other, only somewhat less important, interests emerge through sharing ideas and ideals, which for youth, include new rules concerning the sexual market, value of work, and importance of leisure. Thus, in themselves, tribes motivate participation by offering a rudimentary sub-culture, even if the main motive for participation is to join in the "warm and fuzzy" company of kindred spirits to hear the in-group's music or parade oneself dressed in its characteristic apparel.

Roberts (1997, pp. 9–13), after reviewing the literature in the area, is convinced, despite arguments to the contrary, that youth tribes provide no special identities for their members. Leisure of the kind found in these tribes can enhance self-confidence and help generate positive self-images, but is too superficial and transient to foster a special identity. Instead, youth seem to turn to more traditional ways of identifying themselves, among them class, gender, and sexuality. Still, these identity pegs are more ambiguous today than in the past, but they hold meaning. In short, taste-based tribes organize play and little else, and primarily become attractive for this reason.

In the final analysis, tribes, like the social worlds considered shortly, are seen from the viewpoint of their members as essentially interactive scenes enabling face-to-face relations with at least some other members. This notwithstanding the fact that tribes (and social worlds) are often international in scope, under the banners of which nearly countless numbers of like-minded people assemble, albeit usually only in local organizations. In sociological parlance, they can be said to be operating on the mesostructural plane of social organization.

The term *mesostructure* was coined by David Maines (1982) to signify the intermediate field of interaction lying between the sphere of immediate, face-to-face, social interaction and the sphere of such all-encompassing abstractions as community, society, social class, and large-scale organization. On the mesostructural level, human interaction remains discernible to the people involved as well as in research carried out under the disciplinary banners of sociology, anthropology, and social psychology. A number of studies demonstrate that amateurs, hobbyists, and career volunteers pursue their leisure within some sort of mesostructural context as well as within the four other contexts of personal, interactional, structural, and sociocultural (see Stebbins, 1993d).

Social interaction is an appealing part of tribal life as well as a key component of the playfulness that characterizes that form of leisure organization. It is a different story, however, when it comes to the multitude of social worlds that have emerged in connection with the majority of serious leisure fields. In some respects they look like tribes, for they, too, are mesostructural and, these days, often international in scope. Moreover, they offer enduring friendship mixed with a strong sense of belonging. Yet, organizations at the poles of the structural complexity continuum diverge sharply. They also motivate their members in distinctive ways.

Chapter Six

Social Worlds

Nearly all forms of serious leisure are embedded in a social world, the principal exception being the liberal arts hobbies. These hobbies are, for the most part, individualistic undertakings. Outside the immensely interpersonal enterprise of learning a language, their acquisition rarely requires these hobbyists to enter a social world (even if, as just explained, some do enter tribes). Indeed, hobbyists can seldom find one to enter, a characteristic distinguishing their hobby from other forms of serious leisure. Additionally, some other hobbies and amateur pursuits, among them woodworking, bird-watching, stamp collecting, and piano playing, may be pursued alone, thus isolating a proportion of these enthusiasts from all leisure organizations, networks, small groups, and social worlds. By adopting such a lifestyle, these people are denied, or deny themselves, an important social motive for engaging in these leisure activities.

Expanding the Idea of Social World

The concept of social world was defined and briefly described in Chapter 1, where it was presented as a main component of the unique ethos that helps distinguish serious leisure from its counterpart, casual leisure. But to understand fully its organizational and motivational properties, the idea must now be spelled out in greater detail than was done earlier. Thus every social world contains four types of members: strangers, tourists, regulars, and insiders (Unruh, 1979, 1980). The *strangers* are intermediaries who normally participate a little in the leisure activity itself, but who nonetheless do something important to make it possible. Examples include managing municipal parks (in amateur baseball), minting coins (in hobbyist coin collecting), and organizing the work of teachers' aids (in career volunteering). *Tourists* are temporary participants in a social world; they have come on the scene momentarily for entertainment, diversion, or profit. Most amateur and hobbyist activities have publics of some kind, which are, at bottom, constituted of tourists. The clients of many volunteers can be similarly classified.

Regulars routinely participate in the social world; in serious leisure, they are the amateurs, hobbyists, and volunteers themselves. *Insiders* are those among them who show exceptional devotion to the social world they share, to maintaining it, and to advancing it. Professionals must also be considered insiders in the amateur/professional pursuits. In the studies of amateurs, leisure insiders were analyzed as "devotees" and contrasted with "participants," or regulars (Stebbins, 1992, pp. 46–48).

Missing from Unruh's conceptualization of the social world, yet vital for the study of serious leisure, is the proposition that a vibrant subculture is found there as well, one function of which is to interrelate the "diffuse and amorphous constellations." Consequently, it should be noted that members find a unique set of special norms, values, beliefs, lifestyles, moral principles, performance standards, and similar shared representations associated with each social world. Only by taking these elements into account can we logically speak about, for example, social stratification in social worlds. Unruh treats of stratification when differentiating insiders from regulars, as does Stebbins in serious leisure when differentiating the aforementioned devotees, who are highly dedicated to their pursuit, from participants who are moderately dedicated to it.

Amateur Social Worlds

Yoder's study (1997) of tournament bass fishing in the United States showed, first, that fishers here are amateur sports enthusiasts, not hobbyists (contrary to their earlier classification as "activity participants," Stebbins, 1992, p. 12). Second, he showed that commodity producers serving both amateur and professional tournament fishers play a role significant enough to require modifying the original triangular model of professional-amateur-public (P-A-P) system of relationships on pages 5–6 (see also Appendix, p. 129). In other words, in the social world of these amateurs, some strangers are highly important. They consist, in the main, of national fishing organizations, tournament promoters, and manufacturers and distributors of sporting goods and services. Significant numbers of amateurs make, sell, or advertise commodities for the sport. Professional fishers are supported by commodity agents by means of paid entry fees for tournaments, provision of boats and fishing tackle, and subsidies for living expenses. Top professionals are paid a salary to promote fishing commodities. Yoder's (1997, p. 416) modification results in a more complicated triangular model, consisting of a system of relationships between commodity agents, professionals/ commodity agents, and amateurs/publics (C-PC-AP).

The new C-PC-AP model fits well the social world of stand-up comedy, where certain decisions made by a manager, booking agent, or comedy club owner can weigh heavily on a performer's career (see Stebbins, 1990). It is likewise for certain types of entertainment magicians and their relations with the magic dealers and booking agents who inhabit their social world (Stebbins, 1993c). Finally, Wilson (1995) describes a similar, "symbiotic" relationship between British marathon runners and the mass media. For amateurs in other fields of art, science, sport, and entertainment, who are also linked to sets of strangers operating in their special social worlds, such people play a much more subdued role compared with the four fields just mentioned. Thus for most amateur activities, the simpler, P-A-P model still offers the most valid explanation of their social structure. Mushroom collecting serves as a good example.

Fine (1998) describes the social world of amateur mushroom collectors in the United States. Many are members of local or regional organizations, which often meet weekly during mushrooming season to hear talks, see slide shows, and examine finds that have occurred since they last met. Local clubs also organize several "forays"—mushroom collecting expeditions into nearby fields and forests—for members interested in collecting and eating what they pick. In the United States, many of these clubs are affiliates of the polymorphic North American Mycological Association. Additionally, clubs often hold an annual banquet, an annual picnic, and various get-togethers where members can share dishes prepared from wild mushrooms. Moreover, in some organizations, informal after-meeting gatherings take place at a nearby bar or restaurant, the purpose of which is to continue talk about the shared love for the mushroom and its hunt. Additionally, forays to be held on private property put organizers in touch with landowners.

There is, however, still more to this social world. Budding mushroomers can take classes on fungi, whether offered by the club or by a school, museum, or governmental agency. There is reading to be done, of books and journals kept by the organization or at a nearby public or university library or purchased from bookstores. Many enthusiasts subscribe to

Mushroom, the Journal, a quarterly featuring articles on well-known amateurs and hobbyists in this pursuit, mushrooming forays, evaluations of field guides, and advice on cultivation. Last but not least, are the suppliers of important items of equipment ranging from baskets specially designed for mushroom pickers to microscopes for detailed analysis of finds. In brief, the social world of mushroomers is comprised primarily of strangers, regulars and insiders as well as various organizations, networks, small groups, and a body of literature.

The social world of amateur stand-up comics diverges in many ways from that of amateur mushroom enthusiasts (Stebbins, 1990). For the former, life centers on one or more local comedy clubs, where during "amateur" nights, they are invited to present and polish their acts in five- to ten-minute sets. One of their most important strangers is the club manager (who may also be owner) He, and only rarely she, books budding amateurs for each amateur night and more advanced amateurs for opening "spots" in professional shows, usually held close to and during the weekend. Another important stranger for some comics is the supplier of show business equipment (used, for example, by comic-magicians and musician-comedians). And to be sure, televised comedy and the occasional film about comics make up another part of this social world, as do various annual comedy festivals such as the Festival Juste Pour Rire held in Montreal, Quebec and the U.S. Comedy Arts Festival held in Aspen, Colorado.

Unlike that of mushroomers, the amateur comic's social world has a significant tourist component, notably, the audience. Making them laugh is proof of the entertainer's excellence, which the club manager uses to justify further bookings on amateur nights. Of course, audience laughter is what these amateurs strive for as a major reward of their leisure. Otherwise, regulars and insiders in this field line up along a continuum running from junior to senior comics; that is, from inexperienced amateurs, to those good enough to open professional shows, to various gradations of professional talent, some of which is internationally famous (e.g., Jay Leno, Jerry Seinfeld). Among amateurs, finding tutelage arrangements with professionals or club managers or taking short formal courses, if not both, round out, for the most part, the content of the social world of this serious leisure enthusiast.

Other than the comedy club itself, amateurs in stand-up comedy know little formal organization. The opposite is true, however, for amateur entertainment magicians (Stebbins, 1993c). Many are members of local clubs. Here they have numerous opportunities to perfect parts of their acts before other members (a most critical audience), listen to lectures on magic given by professionals, discuss the strengths and weaknesses of certain pieces of magic apparatus, and at least as important, talk shop about their passion. As already mentioned most local clubs are affiliated with a national or international body, which holds annual conventions, publishes newsletters and magazines, and these days, maintains a lively web site. The most significant strangers for many amateurs are the dealers, owners of shops or mail-order firms who sell various kinds of apparatus, such as cards, sponge balls, mechanical tricks, and stage-appropriate items of apparel like capes and hats.

Like that of comics, the audience at a magic performance is the quintessential tourist element in this social world. It may be composed of adults or children or both. Amateurs, however, do learn entertainment magic much as amateur comics learn their art: through tutelage from professionals and short formal courses from nearby dealers. Magicians are nevertheless considerably more likely to rely on books and manuals to learn particular tricks and generally perfect their acts. Because they are organized with reference to individual arts, the social network and small group facets of the worlds of comedy and magic lack extensive development. By comparison, in many kinds of sport and music, for example (e.g., Apostle, 1992; Finnegan, 1989), amateurs must usually work with others to pursue their interests. Although magic is only rarely presented on television, geographic meccas do exist, most notably, the Magic Castle in Los Angeles and several long-running shows in Las Vegas. Committed amateurs arrange whenever possible to visit these attractions.

Hobbyist Social Worlds

It is possible that research will demonstrate that the most complex social worlds in serious leisure are most likely those of hobbyists. Barbershop singing—classified as activity participation—presents a classic example (Stebbins, 1996a). The vast majority of its enthusiasts belong to a local chapter of one of three all-male or all-female international organizations—SPEBSQSA, Sweet Adelines International, and Harmony Incorporated—and several countries outside North America have their own organizations for men or women. Members typically meet weekly to rehearse in choruses, many of which give annual shows, perform "singouts" (short public or private concerts), and compete. Additionally, some members try to sing in a barbershop quartet as well, which if if of good quality, also performs singouts and competes at conventions. Finally, many chapters hold annual banquets, and invariably following the annual show, an "after glow" (a rollicking postperformance party consisting of food, drink, conversation, and ample barbershop quartet singing).

Some chapter members develop a taste for doing volunteer administrative work for the chapter or its parent organization, for instance, by becoming chapter president or treasurer, coordinator of the annual show, social chair, and the like. The parent organizations, acting as strangers, offer a rich supply of magazines, gift items, pitch pipes, and recorded and written barbershop music. These collectivities set the rules for contests and recruit as well as train judges for evaluating performances. Some experienced choral and quartet singers spend time coaching local and regional groups to help perfect their musical offerings for upcoming shows and contests. A select few are good enough to perform this service for the national organization in weekend workshops sponsored by the regions, districts, and larger local chapters. Many insiders in SPEBSQSA attend Harmony College in Missouri at least once, where for a week in the summer, they polish singing technique, learn how to sight sing, receive ear training, and read about music theory, harmony, and arranging. In all this there is, of course, the all-important tourist, the audience, whose appreciation every chorus and quartet continuously seeks.

Based on research done to date, barbershop can be said to have one of the most evolved social worlds in serious leisure. Other complex hobbyist social worlds have also emerged, one being the making and tinkering hobby of purebred dog breeding. Baldwin and Norris (1999) studied the American Kennel Club (AKC), a polymorphic organization dedicated to advancement of man's best friend through registration and competitive dog shows. The AKC serves as governing body for a large number of local clubs which hold dog shows. The parent organization also trains judges for these shows, at which dog owners often hire an amateur or professional handler skilled in showing dogs. Apart from breeding and raising these animals, owners and other members (some of which no longer have dogs) occasionally serve as volunteers, helping with local club events or, as one of its officers, running the organization. Furthermore, many clubs rent or purchase space for practicing the skills of showing dogs and for conducting community-level training classes.

Baldwin and Norris (1999, p. 8) report that new members, some of whom join more than one dog breeding club, soon acquire a circle of friends whose common passion is breeding dogs, enriching still further their hobbyist social world. Those who become competent judges or handlers develop sizeable networks of contacts in these spheres. The authors also identified four categories of involvement in local AKC affairs (p. 9). *Beginners*—regulars in this social world—have just started participating in formal dog competitions. *Supporters* are on the scene primarily to aid and buttress their spouse's interest in dogs. *Active club members* (insiders) usually fill more than one role, holding a leadership position, traveling to distant competitions, and organizing training classes, to name a few. Lastly, *associates* are former active members who have now reduced their involvement with the club, but nevertheless retain a reputation for skill or for success in competition. In Unruh's classification they would have returned to being regulars.

The AKC itself is a major stranger. It supplies books and videos about dogs, as well as dog-related apparel and artwork. Health and nutritional tips are available to members, as is discussion about canine legislation in the United States. People interested in buying a dog and living harmoniously with their purchase can get advice on these matters from the AKC. Finally, the organization publishes three magazines, one on dogs in general, one on field trials, and one on awards.

The social world of gun collectors is vastly different from the social worlds described to this point. These collectors do not typically form local clubs (although target shooters do); rather their social world revolves around gun auctions and gun shows (Olmsted, 1988). The shows are organized by regional or national gun organizations, however, to which some owners do in fact belong. Collectors like looking at guns, particularly those in which they specialize (e.g., English shotguns, dueling pistols, Civil War weapons), which brings them to the shows. Moreover, they must buy and sell guns to advance their own collections, which draws some of them to auctions. Another aspect of collecting is displaying one's own collection, whether formally at shows or informally at home. In the first, prizes are awarded for best collections and displays thereof. In the second, approbation of the viewer, usually another collector, is reward enough. That guns are sometimes bought and sold outside the auction market and sometimes viewed informally in personal collections, hints at the existence among collectors of networks of contacts consisting of friends and acquaintances with a substantial interest in guns.

Hobbyist collectors of guns, like collectors of many other coveted items, are not to be confused with commercial dealers of these items from whom collectors nonetheless buy on occasion. As a general rule in the collecting hobbies, dealers obtain their stock to make a living through subsequent sales, a motive completely different from that driving hobbyist collectors (Stebbins, 1992, pp. 11–12). Although the latter may try to earn enough money selling a gun (or violin, or painting) to buy one of greater value, they are usually interested only in acquiring a prestigious item for personal and social reasons, or possibly for hedging inflation. Making a living doing this is not their goal.

By the way, casual collecting of such things as matchbooks, beer bottles, and travel pennants is, at best, a marginal instance of hobbyism. Here, there is no equivalent complex of commercial, social, and physical circumstances about which to learn; no substantial aesthetic or technical appreciation possible; no comparable level of understanding of production and use to be acquired. Casual collecting is thus most accurately classified under casual leisure as a kind of play.

Moving on to family history, genealogy has been defended elsewhere as a liberal arts hobby (Stebbins, 2001a, p. 23). In general, since it can usually be carried out alone, this type of serious leisure presents, at best, only a rudimentary social world. Preparing a family history, however, is something of an exception to this rule.

According to Lambert (1995, 1996), women go in for this hobby more often than men. They are attracted to it, in part, by its special social world. For one, family historians enjoy considerable contact with younger genera-tions, to whom they pass on the fruits of their research. They also tend to value meeting present-day relatives, whatever their age, and encounters facilitated by a shared curiosity about common ancestors. Genealogists get acquainted with these relatives through exchanges of letters, telephone calls, the Internet, and sometimes face-to-face interaction. In addition, when using libraries and archives or reading past correspondence written by kin of an earlier era, they expand the boundary of their hobbyist social world beyond the family circle.

Also found beyond the family circle is contact with other genealogists who may advise on technical aspects of conducting this kind of inquiry. Adult education seminars and workshops accomplish the same thing, and do so more systematically. These may be offered by a genealogical society, which some of these hobbyists join specifically for this reason, as well as by a variety of other organizations. Useful information about ancestors can sometimes be obtained from church records, which necessitates getting in touch with people who can give the family historian access to them. Finally, it may be necessary to travel to one or more foreign countries to gain needed information. In sum, the social world of family history is less evolved than some other social worlds considered in this chapter, but it is nevertheless an entity of considerable substance.

The hobbyist sport of curling, whose small group structure was de-scribed in Chapter 2, has its own distinctive social world. Although the four-person curling team is central, it is by no means the only component of this world (Apostle, 1992). Some curlers belong to a curling club, which among its other functions, organizes local, weekend tournaments. Unaffiliated curlers of sufficient skill, be they regulars or insiders, are sometimes invited to play for one of the club teams. Winning teams advance to more inclusive regional or national competitions called bonspiels.

Outside this nucleus, various strangers supply such equipment as brooms, gloves, and special shoes for wearing on ice. Novices can also purchase manuals from these sources which are filled with information on how to play and excel at the game. Apostle (1992, p. 21) notes, too, that some of the more proficient curlers (insiders) circulate among local clubs in search of the best playing opportunities—a practice frowned on by loyal club members. Not least in this social world are the tourists. In Canada, for example, routine tournaments and major bonspiels attract a good deal of attention, and are reasonably well covered by the sports press.

Eldon Snyder (1986), in his study of shuffleboard playing among the elderly in Ohio and Florida, counted at the time 430 active shuffleboard clubs in Florida, 220 in California, with smaller yet significant numbers in many other states. The social world of this sports hobby is similar to that of curling. The International Shuffleboard Association organizes annual competitions that draw players from Japan, Canada, and the United States. This is only the formal side of the hobby; many more men and women play regularly on an informal basis. Whatever the level, players tend to be senior citizens.

As in many of the social worlds considered in this chapter, the world of shuffleboard is populated by both regulars and insiders.

> Within the shuffleboard world the intensity of involvement varies widely. Some senior citizens become consumed by the activities surrounding shuffleboard; for others, involvement lacks intensity and they remain on the periphery of the social world. (Snyder, 1986, p. 239)

The social world of beginners consists, at its core, of lessons, local club tournaments, and from time to time, potluck suppers. Some of these people remain "social players" (regulars), while others push on to become "tournament players" (insiders). Thus in this social world there is a clear leisure career, realized by advancing along lines of knowledge of, skill and experience in the sport. For tournament players, shuffleboard becomes a central life interest, often luring them into multiple contests held nearly every week of the year, some of which are organized in distant communities or parts of the country. These players also make numerous shuffleboard friends in these places as well as at home and for this reason alone live in a more complex hobbyist world than regulars.

Volunteer Social Worlds

As discussion in the preceding chapter suggests, the social worlds of volunteers often revolve around some sort of organization. Volunteer fire departments serve this function extremely well.

Thompson (1997) examined the social world of firefighters volunteering in several departments in southern Alberta, Canada. The many men and few women who comprise them spend most of their volunteer time fighting fires, dealing with automobile accidents, and training for these eventualities. In this core area of this form of leisure, participants are mainly in touch with other members of the same department and with the people affected by the fire or accident they are attempting to manage. They also do other things as well, things that expand their social world

For example, province-wide interdepartmental competitions are held regularly, speed of hose coupling and vehicle extraction being among the more popular. Tourists at these events include not only other firefighters but also members of the general public. Additionally, there are weekly meetings to attend, at which matters like maintenance of the fire hall and fire equipment are discussed. Training may also occur at this time. One of the departments examined by Thompson conducts an annual fundraising campaign for the Muscular Dystrophy Association, which sends its volunteers into the community to drum up interest among merchants and townspeople for participating in a raffle. Some departments must raise money for their own activity-related projects, such as buying a new pumper, leading them to organize such events as dances and car rallies. Moreover, local firefighters get involved in the community's annual celebrations, often by driving their equipment in a parade or staging one or more of the previously mentioned contests. Many departments field a team in the local baseball or curling league.

All the people served by these volunteers can be conceived of as tourists. That is, they benefit in one way or another from firefighter efforts to put out a fire or extract someone from a wrecked car. Or they benefit from the raffles, dances, car rallies, and parade participation of these men and women. Strangers in this social world supply trucks and other equipment as well as firefighter apparel. They include the governmental units that give money to help the departments carry out their services. Regulars and insiders are differentiated by level of knowledge of and experience in executing the more complex and dangerous tasks of this volunteer role.

The author's study of key volunteers serving in francophone grassroots associations in Calgary and Edmonton in Canada revealed that they share a similar though by no means identical social world (Stebbins, 1998b). Their core activities revolve around the association itself, bringing these people in contact primarily with members of the group and the people it serves. Thus, a member of a parents' committee in a francophone school meets with other members of the committee, school personnel, and parents of some of the pupils attending the institution. The president of a francophone chorus interacts mostly with members of the group, but also on occasion with the audience at concerts (tourists).

Nevertheless, key volunteers (insiders), in particular, live in a significantly broader social world than the association's rank-and-file (mostly regulars). Some of the former (often the president and treasurer) must, for example, deal with all sorts of strangers, not the least of which in today's restrictive funding climate are the agencies, both private and governmental, that give supporting funding grants for its projects. Additionally, the treasurer maintains regular contacts with the bank that holds the group's account and all other entities that send bills to the association. Further, some of these associations must deal with suppliers of, for example, music (the chorales), costumes (theater groups), athletic equipment (sports teams), and the like—a task complicated enough to be passed to an appointed key volunteer.

Like volunteer firefighters, key volunteers in francophone grassroots associations must occasionally try to raise money for operating their organization and for certain projects it hopes to pursue. This brings them in contact with the general (largely francophone) public in the local community, as in assisting at a bingo, casino, or silent auction. The search for money may lead to collaboration with one or more other francophone associations in the area, a liaison that usually involves either organizational presidents or key volunteers. All such connections are made with strangers.

A third example of the volunteer's social world comes from Australia, where Harrington, Cuskelly, and Auld (2000) have recently studied this form of serious leisure as pursued in the field of motorsport. Of the three volunteer activities described in this section, motorsport volunteering, to the extent it is limited to races, presents by far the simplest social world. That is, most volunteers here are specialists in an aspect of motorsport, and therefore seem to interact largely, if not exclusively, with one another along with drivers in the race and the entourage of each. For instance, some are flag marshals, point chiefs, or fire marshals, while others serve as pit lane marshals, stewards, and scrutineers. They may be timekeepers and starters or work in a recovery vehicle. Filling such roles does not typically put these volunteers in contact with strangers or tourists, only with each other (as regulars and insiders) and with racers and their personnel, although communicator/media specialists make an obvious exception to this generalization.

Of course, key volunteers are also at work in Australian motorsport. Usually, however, they serve in one of the motorsport organizations, where some play a central role in fundraising or serve on a board of directors. Harrington and her colleagues did not examine these volunteers, though it is likely that, to the extent the latter occupy key positions such as secretary and treasurer, they will find the broad range of contacts with strangers and tourists characteristic of key volunteers described elsewhere in this section. By contrast, rank-and-file members of boards, a number of whom can be considered regulars, appear to operate within quite limited social worlds.

Conclusions

Although their centrality in the lives of individual serious leisure participants varies, formal organizations, if the contents of this chapter are typical, form a noticeable part of nearly every leisure social world. Sure, such collectivities are rather marginal for gun collectors and family historians, and amateur comics are not really members of the comedy clubs in which they perform. Nonetheless, for the rest of the amateur, hobbyist, and volunteer fields considered here, one or more formal organizations form part of the core of their corresponding social worlds. Furthermore, all fields considered here have a tourist component, even though its importance sometimes varies within each (e.g., motorsport volunteering) and at other times varies between them (e.g., gun collecting vis-à-vis stand-up comedy). Otherwise, with respect to the four types of members of social worlds, there appears to be little significant variation across the three kinds of serious leisure: all recognize regulars and insiders, while certain strangers play an indispensable role in facilitating pursuit of the activity in question.

We have yet to analyze the social world of a particular serious leisure activity by exploring all the dimensions and entities that theoretically make it up. Thus we are in no position at this time to say much more about this kind of leisure organization than what has been said in this chapter. Furthermore, small groups (dyads and triads included) and social networks also help comprise the typical leisure social world, but systematic analyses of these are missing as well. The same holds for newsletters, magazines, web sites, mass mailings, and similar mediated means of communication.

Still, the people who make up a given social world and the practices, or patterns of behavior, which have emerged over time have been reasonably well-explored. This has happened not because of systematic research on social worlds (of which there has been very little) but because of the large number and variety of ethnographic studies that have been conducted on the central leisure activities around which they have formed. Yet, for some participants in these activities, the allied social worlds seem more like simple tribes than the complex entities described in this chapter. That is, these participants know that other people share their leisure passion, that some of these people live in the same community and that many more live outside it in the same country or, in many instances, abroad. Moreover, they know these kindred spirits share many of the same leisure habits and values. Thus, amateur astronomers can count on their colleagues, wherever they live, to be perturbed about artificial light pollution, primarily because it interferes with observation of the heavens. Serious stamp collectors the world over expect each other to be connoisseurs of the fine postal cancellations and graphic artwork that distinguish the most collectable postage stamps.

Research has also revealed that, in themselves, serious leisure social worlds, when recognized as such, become attractive formations (Stebbins, 1999, p. 267), though they appear to inspire people more to stay in them than to join them in the first place. Usually, it takes time to learn about the social world of, say, darts or volunteering for the Scouts or Guides, something that really only effectively occurs once inside that world. Nevertheless, belonging to and participating in the social worlds of theater, entertainment magic, stand-up comedy, and classical music were heady experiences for many of the amateurs interviewed. For them, membership and participation constituted two additional powerful reasons for pursuing their art, albeit two social reasons. This is true, in part, because belonging to such a world helps socially locate individual artists in mass urban society as well as helps personalize to some extent their involvement there. Today's serious leisure social world is significantly less impersonal than either the modern mass or the postmodern tribe. Moreover, serious leisure activities generate their own attractive lifestyles, which are associated with particular social worlds.

In fact, nearly every serious leisure activity is anchored in a vibrant social world endowed with the capacity—once recognized—to attract and hold a large proportion of its participants. Although the activity itself is exciting, the excitement it generates is also enhanced by the presence of networks of like-minded regulars and insiders, important strangers, local and national organizations, spaces for pursuing the activity, and tourists who visit from time to time—the audiences, spectators admirers, onlookers, and others. Magazines, newsletters, courses, lectures, workshops, and similar channels of information make up another prominent part of the typical serious leisure enthusiast's social world.

What makes amateur social worlds truly distinct is the indisputable central role that professionals play in them. In some instances these people are available locally, where amateurs can rub elbows with them, pattern their serious leisure lives after them, and marvel at their feats made possible by full-time devotion to the activity. Although not all professionals are good role models or blessed with agreeable personalities, a sufficient number come close enough to these ideals to win a place of honor in one of the worlds of avocational leisure. They may only rarely be seen in person, but their influence is both wide and deep, due in part to their frequent appearance in the print and electronic media.

Finally, remember that here, too, there is also a disagreeable side to their cherished social world for most members. Perhaps a supplier of needed equipment is charging too much for it; perhaps some types of tourists are intolerable (ask any entertainer about how audiences vary); perhaps some ways of doing things or treating others are annoying. For instance, in some fields, amateurs bristle at the way their professional counterparts belittle them. As Stebbins observed, serious leisure is never an unalloyed joy. Still, its rewards are held to significantly outweigh its costs, including those emanating from the relevant social world, participants stay with it, "through thick and thin" as it were.

Social worlds are highly abstract entities, which is why they remain largely invisible to members whose involvement in them is relatively light. Insiders much more than regulars, not to mention neophytes in the activity, get involved often enough across a sufficiently broad range of elements of the social world in question (e.g., small groups, networks, associations, publications, events) to gain a real sense of that formation, abstract as it is. To the extent the activity's social world is not well-perceived by members, it will fail to motivate them to participate, even if they are inspired to participate, perhaps highly, by other organizational forces and the attractiveness of the activity itself.

All the same, the honor of being the most abstract leisure organization must go to the social movement, which motivates participants through the nebulous forces of collective behavior rather than the more concrete sense of belonging to a group, tribe, or social world.

Chapter Seven
Social Movements

Is participation in a social movement a leisure activity? The answer to this
question is both yes and no, for it depends on the movement in question.
Movements abound that gain members through their own volition, suggesting that they freely choose to become involved (the usual limitations of
free choice in leisure apply here). Religious movements provide a set of
examples, as do movements centered on values like physical fitness and
healthy eating. The latter of these values also attract people who feel
pressured by outside forces to participate, such as when their physician
prescribes exercise or weight loss or face an early death. Thus some social
movements are composed of enthusiasts who are there for leisure reasons
and other people who are compelled to be there. Finally, there are movements that would seem to find their impetus primarily in people who feel
driven to champion a particular cause, such as the celebrated temperance
movement of the early twentieth century and the vigorous antismoking
movement of today. A strong sense of obligation fuels their participation.
Those who make up the gun control and nuclear disarmament movements
seem to be cut from the same cloth.

The Nature of Social Movements

Social movements, be they primarily of the leisure variety, the forced variety, or a combination of the two, have left a prominent mark on modern
and postmodern life. A *social movement* is a noninstitutionalized set of
networks, small groups, and formal organizations that has coalesced around
a significant value, which inspires members to promote or resist change
with reference to it. Furthermore, social movements fall under the heading
of *collective behavior:* spontaneous, noninstitutionalized, to some extent

emotional, action of a set of people whose thinking, feeling, and acting are more or less unstructured and, in some instances, impulsive. It is common to classify as collective behavior such phenomena as panics, mobs, riots, and crowds as well as fads, fashions, publics, and social movements. As such this is a sociological rather than a psychological question; the essence of collective behavior is found in the actions of sets of people, not in the acts of isolated individuals.

Several points suggested by these two definitions warrant further consideration. One, social movements are not social groups, but rather networks of groups, organizations, and individuals spanning a community, region, society, and these days with rampant globalization, even much of the world. For individual participants, interaction is therefore possible with only a small proportion of all members of the movement. Two, social movements are fired by an ideology, one function of which is to justify pursuing key values shared by the participants. On the most general plane, these values are initiation or prevention of what they see as important social changes. Three, social movements normally encompass many more people than the typical, usually local, elementary form of collective behavior, for instance a riot or a panic.

Turner and Killian (1987, p. 223) hold that a social movement is, at bottom, a collectivity in that it is "something of an interrelated and coacting unity of persons, rather than a mere aggregate of persons acting separately but in parallel fashion." As such, a social movement is more than a tendency or a trend to, for example, buy certain brands of cars or watch certain types of television programs, something usually done by aggregates of people acting separately but in parallel. Finally, movements are comprised of acting individuals, which excludes those who accept movement values but do nothing to help realize them.

Types of Social Movements

In an area rife with typologies, David Aberle's (1966) fourfold classification of social movements is still considered one of the most useful and comprehensive. It is constructed along two dimensions: *locus* and *amount* of desired change. Concerning the first, some movements strive to change individuals while others strive to change the social order. The amount of change sought may be partial or total. Cross-classifying these two dimensions results in four types of movements labeled by Aberle as transformative, reformative, redemptive, and alternative.

Transformative movements seek total or near total change in the social order. It can be argued that the scope of the women's movement is of this magnitude. Its proponents have worked for better than a century to create equality for females in every walk of life: legal, political, religious, familial, and educational. Men and women have also striven for equal treatment of both sexes in sport, at work, and in various leisure activities. Many would say that, since the battle has not been fully won, the movement will persist.

Reformative movements aim for partial change of the social order. Many of them work toward some sort of social reform, with the antiabortion and environmentalist movements being prime examples. The campaign for nuclear disarmament is reformative in nature. In fact, the list of contemporary reformative movements is long.

Redemptive movements seek to effect total change in individuals. Here the inner condition of people is believed to need modification; the proposed modification is looked on as a way of solving some personal or social problem.

The New Age Movement provides a modern example (Melton, 1986, pp. 107–124). It began in the early 1970s in an attempt to blend certain Eastern and mystical religions (e.g., Islam, Buddhism, Hinduism) with the religious disenchantment of many Westerners. The central aim of the New Age is to transform the individual through use of special mystical systems of thought. New ways of looking at the world are taught, such as by discovering psychic abilities, experiencing physical and psychological healing, realizing new personal potentials, and finding intimate involvement in a community. Melton (1986, p. 113) expresses the vision of the New Age: It is a "world transformed, a heaven on earth, a society in which the problems of today are overcome and a new existence emerges." Individual members assume that a basic energy exists (an energy different from light or heat) that underlies and penetrates all existence. It is this energy that spawns new ways of looking on the world. Among the groups and organizations that count themselves as part of the New Age Movement are the Divine Light Mission, Transcendental Meditation, Tantric yoga groups, Zen Buddhism, the Tara Center, and the Unity School of Christianity.

Alternative movements seek partial change in people. The current yen for weight loss, physical fitness, and smoking cessation, which appear to have reached movement-like proportions, are examples. The antismoking movement has at least two components. One is made up of people trying to quit smoking. They avail themselves of various kinds of assistance, including medical advice, self-help groups, personal programs, and pharmaceutical aids. The other component is comprised of people opposed to smoking in the presence of nonsmokers. They lobby for restrictions on smoking in public places, forbid it in their homes and offices, and even campaign for higher tobacco taxes on the belief such as measure will help curb this practice.

Participation in Movements

As Zurcher and Snow (1981, pp. 449–464) point out, an individual's decision to participate in a movement initially and over time is affected by several interrelated conditions: movement ideology, social network contacts, commitment to the movement, and conversion to its ideology. Sociologists and psychologists have also identified a variety of motives for joining social movements. Pinard and Hamilton (1986, pp. 229–232) list six: deprivations, aspirations, moral obligations, collective incentives, selective incentives, and expectations of success. The first three are personal, or internal, motives. Here a deprivation is a grievance that goads people into action (e.g., polluted environment, gender inequality, availability of abortion on demand). By contrast, an aspiration is a value that many individuals want but have been unduly denied. A smoke-free working environment is an aspiration for some people. Whether motivated by deprivations or aspirations, members of a movement, by dint of its ideology, feel morally obligated to participate in it.

Selective incentives are the special rewards that sometimes come with participation in a movement, such as power, money, and recognition given to individual movement members to encourage active involvement. Still, collective incentives may be all that is required to obtain participation from most people. These include praise, gratitude, and feelings of involvement. In the end, all these motives depend on the expectation that personal participation will result in movement success.

Zurcher and Snow (1986) reviewed a number of studies showing that most people who join a social movement learn of it through their social network contacts with participants already in the movement. Directly or indirectly, many recruits know someone who is active in the movement. Moreover, networks serve as information pipelines through which outsiders learn of a movement's ideology and its goals.

Additionally, the conditions of commitment and conversion help explain participation in social movements (Snow and Machalek, 1984, p. 171). These authors report that strength of commitment has been found to vary from member to member, although a high degree of commitment leads to faithful participation among those so oriented. As for conversion, it bolsters commitment, whether to a religious movement or to one centered on political or moral concerns.

Kleidman (1994) reviewed research showing that three basic patterns of professionalism influence volunteer activism in social movements: professionals may inhibit if not erode activism or they may replace it or facilitate it. His research on peace movement organizations in the United States demonstrates, contrary to other studies on the matter, that social movement organizations are likely to present a combination of all three patterns. Professionalism refers to use of paid staff supported by internal sources or outside sources or both. In this literature, these people fill leadership and decision-making roles. Professionals inhibit volunteer activism by discouraging participation by members or by avoiding political strategies that require grassroots mobilization. On the other hand, professionals sometimes facilitate volunteer activism when it flags. They can also increase volunteer effectiveness. In replacement, professionals change the organization such that it no longer needs volunteer help.

Social Movement Organizations

Although social movements may start as crowds—as elementary collective behavior—they cannot last in this form. Turner and Killian observe that

> because social movements are sustained rather than transitory, they require stable organization and leadership and stable constituencies form which adherents can be constantly recruited and replaced. (1987, p. 242)

Moreover, some movements are planned; here volunteer organizations, perhaps preceded by a grassroots association, begin early on to play a major role. As the history of a social movement and its organizations unfolds, its initial, often charismatic, leaders are replaced by a more bureaucratic type. Charismatic leaders rule by dint of their commanding personal qualities, which attract devoted followers over whom the leaders have exceptional influence and control. Departure of such figures, as by retirement or death, commonly sparks major changes in the movement. No one can fill the shoes of these leaders. Charisma must now be routinized: leadership must be transformed into a set of bureaucratic, or institutionalized, roles.

During this transition, a decline in membership may occur, as those once attracted more to the leader than the movement drift away. Moreover, the power vacuum left by the leader's departure may engender factionalism and power struggles among that person's lieutenants. Finally, at least at the organizational level, there is during transition a trend toward bureaucratization (i.e., proliferation of roles, rules, formal positions) and another toward professionalism of the executive core (e.g., lengthy formal training, remunerated work, established performance criteria, recognized authority).

Social Movement Participation as Leisure

Although an overstatement to argue that all people participating in social movements do so in their leisure, as do McCarthy and Zald (1987, pp. 337–392), it is clear that some movements are primarily expressions of leisure involvement. As already mentioned, participation driven by strongly held negative emotions such as fear, hate, disgust, and revenge overrides the definition of leisure as uncoerced activity, which turns this kind of potential free time involvement into forced action carried out in obligated time. For social movement participation to be of the leisure variety, it must be undertaken because members positively want to do it, not because they negatively feel they have to do it, that is, feel pressured. The emotions evoked, then, should be on the order of love, joy, happiness, and the like.

Participation as leisure seems amply evident in movements propelled by goals like self or community development, realization of aesthetic values, or creation of a better life. These movements, when truly leisure, are *additive*. That is, they do not reach their goals by first eliminating something. By this logic the antismoking movement is actually *subtractive*; even though it aims to improve the air we breath (an aesthetic value). It is founded on fear of, and therefore need to eliminate, carcinogenic tobacco smoke. It is likewise with those political movements whose goals are to control hated or feared ethnic or deviant groups, even though movement success would lead to a better life for participants because the object of such sentiments would be in some significant way contained.

The four types of movements set out earlier are illustrated next. Each example portrays a positive emotional involvement for the large majority of participants. These participants find leisure in movement-related activities undertaken as individuals as well as members of groups, networks, and organizations. Moreover in this instance, being part of the movement itself constitutes the unique motivational force. As we have observed, being in a group or network is motivating in its own right, whereas being in one that is also part of a social movement adds something special. Moreover, the distinctive goals and values of the latter give membership in the former further meaning, since it is accompanied by a particular identity based on shared "we-ness" and "groupness" that comes with participation there (Beaford, Gongaware & Valadez, 2000, p. 2721).

Transformative Movements

One colorful example of this type of movement is the millennial or chiliastic movement, whose members declare that for one thousand years (a millennium) holiness will triumph and Christ will reign on earth. This period will start with Christ's appearance in visible form in this world. In 1968 evangelist David Berg organized a group of California teenagers that became the nucleus of a movement dubbed by the press as "The Children of God." Intense hostility in the United States has since driven most adherents to Europe, Africa, and South America. From these locations they espouse the Second Coming of Christ, along with total transformation of present-day society as we know it. The following list of beliefs was excerpted in May 2001 from the movement's web site (http://www.thefamily.org):

> We believe that we are now living in the time period known in Scripture as the "Last Days" or the "Time of the End;" that is, the era which immediately precedes the Second Coming of Jesus Christ, when "the kingdoms of this world are [to] become the Kingdom of our Lord, and of His Christ; and He shall reign forever and ever" (Revelation 11:15). In brief, a careful analysis of Biblical prophecy has led us to embrace the following beliefs:
>
> (a) Prophecy Fulfilled: Many Biblical prophecies and "signs of the times" that specifically predict world conditions prior to Christ's Second Coming have unerringly been fulfilled within our generation, confirming that we are indeed living in the Last Days. "As it was in the days of Noah, so shall also the coming of the Son of Man be" (Matthew 24:37), for "evil men and seducers shall wax [grow] worse and worse, deceiving and being deceived" (2 Timothy 3:13; see also Matthew 16:3; Matthew 24; 2 Timothy 3:1–7.)

(b) The Antichrist: Seven years before Jesus' Return, a powerful world leader known in Scripture as the "Beast," "Man of Sin," "Son of Perdition" or "Antichrist," will surreptitiously rise to power, gaining sufficient influence to "confirm a covenant" [peace treaty] (Daniel 9:27) with the primary antagonists in the Mideast, focusing on the centre of the crisis, Jerusalem.... (see 1 John 2:18; 2 Thessalonians 2:1–4, 9; Revelation 13:4,7.)

(c) Great Tribulation: Three-and-a-half years after this peace initiative, the Satan-possessed Antichrist will break the covenant, abolish Jewish temple worship, declare that he alone is God, and demand all the world's veneration and worship. At this time he will institute a universal credit system, whereby none will be legally permitted to buy or sell essential goods, except those who bear this demagogue's mark or number, the "Mark of the Beast," in their right hand or forehead. These events will plunge the entire world into an unprecedented time of social chaos and religious persecution.... (see Daniel 9:27; 11:31; 2 Thessalonians 2:4; Matthew 24:15,21; Revelation 11:3–6; 13:7; 12:11.)

(d) The Second Coming of Christ: The three-and-a-half-year period of Great Tribulation will be climaxed by the return of Jesus Christ to the Earth... All of the born-again believers will then be supernaturally delivered from their cruel persecutors by means of the Rapture, the miraculous event whereby their bodies will be gloriously translated and made like Jesus' Own resurrection body, as they rise to meet the Lord in the air.... (1 Thessalonians 4:16,17; see also Matthew 24:29,30; Revelation 1:7; 1 Corinthians 15:51,52; Philippians 3:20,21.)

(e) The Marriage Supper, the Wrath of God, and the Battle of Armageddon: Following their Rapture and Resurrection, the saved will partake of the glorious "Marriage Supper of the Lamb" in Heaven, and appear before the Judgment Seat of Christ for rewards of service rendered on Earth. Meanwhile, God's angels of judgment will pour out His plagues and wrath upon the Antichrist and his followers, culminating in the Battle of Armageddon, when Jesus and the hosts of Heaven return to utterly defeat and destroy the Satanic Antichrist and his evil hordes. (see Revelation 7:9,13–

17; chapter 19; 2 Corinthians 5:10; Daniel 12:2,3; Revelation 14:9,10; 16:1–21.)

(f) Christ's Millennial Reign: Jesus Christ and His victorious Heavenly forces will then occupy and assume absolute control of the entire world, ruling and reigning over the survivors of Armageddon, and establishing the Kingdom of God on Earth. Justice, equity and true righteousness will at last prevail.... (see Daniel 2:44; Revelation 20:1–4,6; 5:10; Isaiah 2:2–4; 11:6–9; Psalm 46:9; Jeremiah 31:34.)

(g) The Battle of Gog and Magog/The New Heavens and the New Earth: After the thousand years of the Millennial era have expired, Satan will be released from his prison for "a little season" (Revelation 20:3,7), to deceive those survivors of Armageddon who have refused to willingly submit to the Lordship of Christ and His reign of righteousness. These unregenerate rebels will again follow Satan.... (see Revelation 20:7–9; 2 Peter 3:10–13; Isaiah 40:4.)

(h) The White Throne Judgment: The unsaved dead of all ages will then be raised to appear before God at the awesome "Great White Throne Judgment," which is...described in the Book of Revelation (Revelation 20:11,12,15).

(i) New Jerusalem: God's marvelous Heavenly City, New Jerusalem, will then descend like a stupendous jewel from above to crown the paradisiacal New Earth. The Heavenly City is the glorious eternal Heavenly home for all of God's saved children, the hope of all ages, where at last, "the tabernacle of God is with men, and He will dwell with them, and they shall be His people, and God Himself shall be with them, and be their God. And God shall wipe away all tears from their eyes; and there shall be no more death, neither sorrow, nor crying, neither shall there be any more pain: for the former things are passed away" (Revelation 21:3,4; see also the remaining verses of Revelation Chs. 21 and 22.)

Where is the leisure component in this social movement? Much of it, it appears, is ordinary leisure, leisure activity of everyday life, undertaken in this instance in the course of communal living. Some of it, it turns out, is found in the sphere of sexuality, for in his later thought Berg held that his Children of God should assume the role of harbinger of the new loving society by being its foremost living examples (Melton, 1986, p. 156). He assigned the Children a new sexual ethic in which love and sex were equated and free expression of sexuality, including incest, fornication, adultery, lesbianism (though not male homosexuality), was not only allowed but also encouraged. Such libertarianism eventuated in a most unsavory public image for the movement, which in 1979, forced Berg to change its name to Family of Love and still later to that of The Family. The Family now claims 12,000 members living in 1,400 centers in more than 100 countries (The Family, 2001).

Reformative Movements

The environmental movement revolves around questions related to protection of the world's physical environment. It illustrates well how participation in a reformative movement can be seen as leisure for the majority of followers. True, many in this movement do little more than write the occasional letter to a newspaper or a politician expressing their particular environmental concerns or, more rarely, contribute money for advancement of environmentalist goals. Such activity is too sporadic to be regarded as leisure in the sense that is being explored in this book, however, and is therefore not considered in this section.

True leisure-based participation in the environmental movement is evident when, for example, members regularly get together to clean up the shores of a lake or ditches along a stretch of highway, perform maintenance on hiking trails, or save particular species of wildlife. Some of these people expand their involvement in the movement by attending meetings of organizations the mission of which is to work up proposals for solving pressing environmental problems. Others help with routine but vital clerical services (e.g., preparing mailings, phoning members about environmental issues or financial contributions). There is also constant need in environmentalist organizations for the talents of bookkeepers and administrative assistants, which some volunteers meet as part of their leisure.

Like other movements, the environmental movement is organized and held together in part by various means of communication. Thus someone— normally a volunteer—must routinely prepare newsletters and update web sites. Moreover, many environmental organizations are run by boards of directors and a small number of subordinate managers, all of whom are likely to be volunteers. Other personnel are needed to represent the movement, in general, and the organization, in particular, at local fairs, civic celebrations, and similar community events. Finally, some environmental organizations hold events of their own (e.g., road races, silent auctions), which absorb considerable time and effort of volunteer members attracted to this kind of activity.

In Quebec, for instance, citizens concerned about the environmental fate of the Saint Lawrence River have joined committees formed to manage government-established Priority Intervention Zones (ZIPs) of the river. Each ZIP committee is composed of local citizens working together to identify their priorities for riverine improvement and plans for achieving them. These committees also meet with representatives of environmental and industrial groups, elected politicians, civil servants as well as fellow citizens to work out through discussion and consensus an approach to improving the quality of the Saint Lawrence acceptable to all (Lepage, 2001).

Redemptive Movements

The New Age Movement provides many a modern example of the redemptive type of social movement (Melton, 1986, pp. 107–124). Let us consider the International Society for Krishna Consciousness (ISKCON). Known colloquially as the Hare Krishna Movement, this Eastern religion has taken root in North America and elsewhere in the Western world, albeit in considerably modified form. It provides a concrete example of the leisure element in the New Age Movement. Its adepts are conspicuous on city streets where, with heads shaven (except for a tuft of hair), wearing traditional clothing, and chanting their mantra, they solicit money for the religion. The Movement was founded in New York in 1965 by His Divine Grace A.C. Bhaktivedanta, Swami Prabhupada. Hare Krishnas are followers of the Vaisnava tradition of the Hindu religion. Lord Krishna is held to be the ultimate manifestation of the creator god, Brahman, who is the central godhead figure in all forms of Hinduism. Down through the centuries the belief became established that chanting, singing, and dancing are the best ways to rid the soul of ignorance and bad karma (predestined failure) and thereby to gain salvation. Chanting, singing, and dancing are seen as direct expressions of love for Lord Krishna.

When Swami Prabhupada brought the Vaisnava tradition to the United States in the 1960s, the atmosphere generated by the counterculture of the time was ripe for his message, according to Stoner and Parke (1977, pp. 44–45) and Melton (1992, p. 234). The swami taught that the world is on the road to inevitable decline, which, however, will not culminate for nearly a half million years. The singing and dancing of the Hare Krishnas will help them avoid this decline. In the end, Lord Krishna will return to Earth and save his devotees. As for the rest of humanity, its destiny is destruction.

Unlike the practice in India, where followers are born into this religion, North American Hare Krishnas are recruited from the general population. They follow a strict spiritual life in the centers and special farms of ISKCON, many of them located in Canada, the United States, and cities and towns elsewhere in the world (*Back to Godhead*, 1982, pp. 30–31). Since food is an important part of Hare Krishna credo, a Krishna vegetarian restaurant or two are commonly found in larger cities everywhere.

By chanting the *maha-mantra*—Hare Krishna, Hare Krishna, Krishna Krishna, Hare Hare/Hare Rama, Hare Rama, Rama Rama, Hare Hare—the Krishnas hope to reach the mature stage of love of God, where believers and God come together. Other principles of the religion include the following:

- By sincerely cultivating a bona fide spiritual science, we can be free from anxiety and come to a state of pure, unending, blissful consciousness.

- We are not our bodies but eternal spirit souls, part and parcel of God (Krishna). As such we are all brothers and sisters, and Krishna is ultimately our common father.

Alternative Movements

Perhaps no alternative movement in Western culture has these days as high a profile as the physical fitness movement, which for many participants has to do with either losing weight or maintaining it. There are two basic types of physical fitness: health-related and motor-related. Despite some overlap between the two, major differences separate them. Health-related physical fitness is primarily influenced by a person's exercise habits. Thus it is a dynamic state subject to change. Characteristics determining health-related physical fitness include strength and endurance of skeletal muscles, joint flexibility, body composition, and cardiorespiratory endurance.

Motor-performance physical fitness refers to ability of the neuromuscular system to carry out specific tasks. Special tests are used to assess this type of fitness. The major health-related characteristics measured by these tests are strength and endurance of the skeletal muscles and speed or power of the legs.

Exercise contributes to overall bodily fitness. An adequate exercise program is necessary to maintain physical and emotional fitness and to deal effectively with everyday stress. The body's ability to adjust to stress is linked to physical fitness, which is one reason proponents of such activity give for seeking this sort of personal change in the world's population.

The vast majority of people in the fitness movement participate in it by doing little more than their fitness activities and, for a significant proportion of this group, maintaining a healthy diet. To be sure, many also talk with friends and relatives about these activities, their pleasures, their benefits, and in some instances, their costs, as when one of them overdoes it and pulls a muscle or breaks a limb. Note, however, that by no means all members of this movement define fitness as leisure. For exercise routines are seen by some people as woefully tedious, if not painful, something they do reluctantly on orders from a physician or the good advice of a respected book or periodical, to mention but a few of many incitements to bodily perfection that abound in our age.

Furthermore, an unknown but significant proportion of members of the fitness movement go beyond their exercise programs to serve as watchdogs for ensuring availability of fitness installations (e.g., gymnasiums, swimming pools, sports courts, cycling, walking paths) and time in which to use of them. That is, they speak with employers about such matters as well as with governmental officials and facility administrators, and they must often contact these people several times to obtain the desired result, if even they do manage to succeed. Maintaining personal physical fitness is made even more difficult, although usually not impossible, when facilities are nonexistent or in short supply or time to use them is severely limited.

Additionally, some members of this movement serve as volunteers in one of their community's (noncommercial) fitness centers. Here they may serve on the board of directors or fill an administrative or managerial post. Other volunteer roles include promoting the center and perhaps helping with some of its maintenance needs.

Finally, fitness enthusiasts may volunteer to help disadvantaged groups become fit, among them the elderly and people with physical handicaps. Though professionally trained personnel are normally hired to initiate such people into particular, appropriate activities and to help them maintain their involvement here, volunteers can assist with simple exercise, such as taking them for a walk or working with them in routine calisthenics. These occasions also give lay fitness devotees another opportunity to promote their passion and justify its importance.

Conclusions

Few people would think of joining a social movement as a conscious strategy for enhancing their leisure lifestyle. Nor would the typical leisure counselor think of advising clients that such formations could be an exciting way to pass their free time. Nevertheless, each year hundreds of thousands of people around the world do join social movements, in many instances convinced by friends or relatives (network contacts) that their participation in one or another of them is important. Sometimes their influence is ethical; they argue the potential recruit has a duty to work for the movement. This person should feel obliged to become involved. Yet obligation presented this way is not leisure or is, at most, a marginal instance of it (Stebbins, 2000b).

Still, other people are recruited on the basis of pleasant images about a given movement and its activities beamed their way by intimates and acquaintances. Perhaps there is also an obligatory element here—a duty—but if so, it is nonetheless framed in predominantly enjoyable or satisfying terms as leisure activity of the casual or serious kind. For these people working to help reach movement goals and realize movement values has its genuinely appealing side, which is simply unavailable in any other form of leisure organization, including these days traditional political parties (Rojek, 2001, pp. 118–119). Thus, the movement-related leisure of The Family is distinctive precisely because it is undertaken with other members of that social movement. Engaging in physical exercise is enjoyable in part because people know that, by doing this, they are reaffirming values shared with millions of like-minded participants across the world. In this sense, the motivational impetus of tribes and social movements is much the same.

Chapter Eight
Implications

This book has revolved, in the main, around the proposition that leisure participation is motivated not only by psychological but also by social conditions, with many of the latter being organizational in character. Here, as in most other areas of life, action is structured, or organized, in dyads, small groups, social networks, and grassroots associations as well as in larger, more complex organizations and, still more broadly, in social worlds and social movements. It has been argued further that much can be learned about why people participate in leisure, in general, and certain leisure activities, in particular, by studying the social organization of this sphere of social life.

A number of practical implications issue from this exploration of motivational features of leisure organizations. Most of these implications are related to leisure education, the subject of the following section. Some also bear on optimal leisure lifestyle; they are taken up next. The chapter closes on a moderately polemical note, served up in an examination of Robert Putnam's bowling alone thesis as it bears on organized leisure, civil society, and capacity of the first to motivate people to participate in the second. It is noted that certain personal strategies for pursuing leisure in everyday life occasionally affect participation in leisure organizations and in this way indirectly leave their mark on civil society.

Implications for Leisure Education

The main themes of this book relate directly to the goal of leisure education, a profession that also includes leisure counseling and leisure volunteering. Leisure education has, among other goals, helped children and adults achieve an optimal leisure lifestyle, which as mentioned at the start, refers to a judicious balance of serious and casual leisure. Whereas serious leisure must often be taught to those who would take it up (or they must teach themselves), casual leisure, for the most part, comes with no such requirement. Nevertheless, leisure educators must still emphasize that some measure of casual leisure is important for well-being, for it is in such activity that people relax (Kleiber, 2000), play creatively with things and ideas (Moreno, 2000), and generally enjoy life without significant effort (Stebbins, 2001c).

To the extent that educating people for leisure involves encouraging them to go in for particular leisure activities, the instructors, counselors, and volunteers in this endeavor will also want to note for the people they serve (e.g., students, clients) the motivational features of the various leisure organizations involved. Thus it is not evident to everyone that small groups of all sizes create their own idiocultures, described earlier as distinctive sets of shared ideas that emerge with reference to them. Idioculture is local culture, developed within and as an expression of an actual small group. It consists of a system of knowledge, beliefs, behaviors, and customs peculiar to the collectivity, which leisure educators can describe as being most exciting to be privy to. Being an insider has its singular appeal.

Turning first to leisure dyads, their interpersonal quality makes them especially enticing. Here exists a high level of deeply satisfying intimacy and interaction gained through continuous interchanges between two people. This was qualified in Chapter 2 as relational leisure. Still, it is much the same with larger small groups. Individual members of these collectivities have, in most instances, positive emotional attachments to each other and are known to one another as whole personalities rather than, in a much more limited way, as partial individuals filling specialized roles. Recognizing the idioculture of a dyad or other small group contributes to perceiving that entity as unique among all other entities of the same kind (us vis-à-vis them).

Serious leisure takes on some special qualities when pursued in small groups. For instance, people do establish or join ongoing small music ensembles, sports teams, hobbyist groups, or volunteer service units. Here, in contrast to their casual leisure interests, they typically participate by enacting specialized roles that together form a larger whole, such as performing a jazz tune or playing a basketball game. Here, too, personal identity hinges not only on group membership but also on how well individuals carry out these roles. Thus membership in a serious leisure group, unlike that in a casual leisure group, brings recognition for the acquired skills, knowledge, and experience needed to execute the activity in question well. As before, leisure instructors, counselors, and volunteers would do well to indicate that these special features of small-group life constitute important reasons for taking up activities of this kind.

Further, as individuals pursue their leisure interests, they develop networks of contacts (family, friends, and acquaintances) related in different ways to those interests. As a person develops more interests, the number of networks grows, bearing in mind that members of some of these will likely overlap at times. The strength of network ties is often important, for it has been shown that people tend to engage in leisure with significant others, and people with whom they have strong ties. Leisure educators would do well to describe how appealing involvement in networks can actually be (this harmonizes with the positive connotation of networking) and to encourage would-be leisure participants to pursue collective leisure with those with whom they have strong ties.

Grassroots Associations

The several motivational properties of grassroots associations set out in Chapter 3 also combine into an important set of principles worthy of dissemination through leisure education. People served thus could be informed that, in themselves, these associations offer many interesting activities and experiences, all being good reasons for taking up the leisure they organize by joining the appropriate group.

Although altruism and self-interestedness, in diverse combinations, are the basic motives here, secondary motives, like all motives, also initiate, pattern, time, and direct action. The latter were considered in Chapter 3 under the heading of "incentives," the most important of them being the sociability and purposive types. The first refers to the satisfaction members receive from being in the company of and interacting with other members and clients of the association and from friendships and acquaintanceships that develop along the way. Purposive incentives bring satisfaction through realizing group goals, achieved in ways that harmonize with its ideology about what the goals should be and how they should be reached.

Seven other incentives that motivate members of grassroots associations, depending on the nature of the group and the needs of individual members. Service incentives are of two kinds: helping the association's clients and helping other members. Informational incentives are at work when people join an association to gain knowledge about something. People seeking personal growth have a developmental incentive for seeking membership in a particular grassroots association, often a self-help group.

Members of these organizations sometimes join for utilitarian reasons. For some the motive is material, remunerative, or occupational, while for others it is professional or economic. Opportunities provided by the group for making business contacts, getting inside connections to a job, or obtaining free passes to artistic events exemplify this incentive. The charismatic incentive helps explain why people join grassroots associations to be led by or work along side a highly attractive and influential personality. Akin to the purposive incentive is the lobbying incentive, as expressed in advocacy and representation to government. Usually such activity takes place on a regional or national plane, however, well beyond the scope of the typical local group. Last on the list, although hardly least, is the prestige incentive. It is an honor to be a member, and even more honorable to be an officer, of an exclusive establishment like one of the city's elite country clubs or business organizations.

Several features of life in grassroots associations further account for participation there. Following the work of Bishop and Hoggett (1986) we examined three: leisure subcultures, contributions of individual members, and handling member diversity. The first two have import for leisure education.

The subculture of grassroots associations is the analog of the idioculture of small groups, and in fact, when associations are of small group size, the two are one and the same. For associational subculture is also local, developed within and as an expression of an actual collectivity. It, too, consists of a system of knowledge, beliefs, behaviors, and customs peculiar to the group. Members use this system when interacting with one another, and expect to be understood by the others. Knowing the subculture and using it as interactive code is enjoyable in itself, still another reason for being in the group and pursuing the activities it organizes. As with small groups, being an insider in a grassroots association has its own appeal, something leisure educators should certainly take note of.

When we examined the incentives people have for joining grassroots associations, we also considered, to a certain extent, the contributions individuals make to them. That is, someone who joins a group in search of sociability contributes to this side of group life while realizing a main personal goal. Similarly, a person enamored of the services an organization offers—for instance conducting guided tours of an old church or maintaining hiking trails—contributes to it by helping provide those services. It bears repeating here that possibly nowhere else in the vast world of leisure and voluntary action are personal and collective interests so finely meshed, and possibly nowhere else are the motives of altruism and self-interestedness so closely intertwined.

Fine (1989), in his theory of provisioning for leisure, highlights the importance of key resources for engaging in particular free-time activities. These resources are provided by a wide variety of organizations. Individual interest in a given activity, he observes, depends at least as much on the latter being available and having a reputation of being fun as on personal need and preference. Leisure educators can help the people they serve find organizations capable of providing the resources they need to engage effectively in their chosen leisure activities.

Specifically, these educators would do well to discuss Fine's four key resources of leisure organizations, as these bear on particular interests of the people they serve. The first is knowledge, information that enables competent execution of the leisure activity. The second is sociability, and many clubs offer various "sociable times" during a typical year, including dinners, picnics, parties, and receptions. Additionally, successful organizations allow time for informal interaction among members when they attend meetings and other official get-togethers. Many leisure activities have their own identity symbols (e.g., a cap, T-shirt, lapel pin, bumper sticker), and it is often left to organizations to provide them. In prestigious organizations, the membership card is a primary identity symbol. Fourth, some leisure resources are copyrighted and made available only through an organization, as happens with choral arrangements obtained from the barbershop societies and trail guides published by certain hiking clubs.

Volunteer and Leisure Service Organizations

Leisure educators, in discussing with their students and clients the attractive qualities of volunteer and leisure service organizations, might note, as was done in Chapter 4, that volunteer organizations are distinguished by two criteria. One is that they rely heavily on paid staff. The other is that they are established to work for a cause or provide a service rather than to pursue a pastime. They nonetheless depend significantly on volunteer help to reach their goals. By contrast, leisure service organizations are not voluntary groups. Rather, they are collectivities consisting of paid staff who provide one of more leisure services to a targeted clientele. To be sure, their clients are engaging in particular leisure activities, but the organizations providing them are not themselves leisure organizations of the sort considered in this book. Leisure service organizations are established either to make a profit, or more simply, to make enough money to continue to exist and provide their services. Let us turn first to volunteer organizations and their implications for leisure education.

Volunteer organizations, as the term indicates, offer a leisure outlet for volunteers, some of it casual, some of it of the career variety. Organizations like religious establishments, seniors' centers, and political parties engage large numbers of both types. Compare this with organizations like hospitals, primary schools, and the Peace Corps that rely almost exclusively on career volunteers. Furthermore, some volunteer organizations need, for the most part, only casual help; they include community food banks, the Salvation Army, and groups established to provide transportation for the elderly. As for amateurs and hobbyists, they rarely, if ever, form volunteer organizations, although polymorphic structures in these two types of leisure commonly include such organizations at the national or international level. They set guidelines as well as offer important services for constituent grassroots associations operating locally.

In addition to all this, leisure educators will want to inform the people they serve about some of Pearce's (1993) findings. She observed, for example, that feelings of personal importance to an organization and extensive social involvement with its members (both paid staff and other volunteers) were rewards of sufficient appeal to generate substantial commitment to the organization. People must know they can find such rewards in volunteer organizations, while it is also incumbent on volunteer managers there to ensure that the rewards can be experienced. This latter requirement is not, however, a matter for leisure education.

Turning now to leisure service organizations, we consider Godbey's (1999) typology. Educators can use his taxonomy to apprize those interested in one of these services of the many possibilities from which they may choose. Thus the neutral provider attempts to identify and supply leisure experiences in which certain groups of people want to participate. Municipal parks and recreation departments operate at times in this capacity. Other service organizations act as change agents that offer activities in which their directors believe people should be involved. Some leisure service organizations are coordinators of leisure opportunities. Schools, municipal park and recreation departments, YMCAs and YWCAs do this. Additionally, organizations are established to provide leisure for the recreationally dependent, for example, people who are poor or have handicaps.

Other organizations—the most pervasive in the leisure service field (Godbey, 1999, p. 361)—are for-profit establishments. One type promotes specific leisure activities and facilities, such as bowling centers, skating arenas, golf courses and bingo halls. Services that enhance the physical environment intend to provide a good boating, fishing, hunting, or camping experience. Related to the change agents are the health promoters; they organize activities for people who yearn to improve their health and physical conditioning. Nonetheless, their clients need no persuading in this regard, only an opportunity to pursue this kind of leisure, whereas the clients of change agents have to be encouraged to take up the leisure being offered. Some organizations—among them Elderhostel and programs in continuing education—provide leisure education, offering this service across a great range of amateur and hobbyist activities. Finally, promoters and facilitators of tourism sell one of the most sought after forms of leisure in the twenty-first century.

Also pointed out in Chapter 4, although there are no studies of motivation to participate in leisure education as provided by a leisure service organization, a handful of general observations have been made. These sketch some of the motivational links between individual participants and, say, a community adult education program. Selman, Cooke, Selman, and Dampier (1998) list four functions of adult education as seen by its clients, three of which—the social (roles in community), recreational, and self-developmental functions—bear directly on leisure and leisure education. That is, through learning and consonant with these functions, the authors see adult education as contributing to the maintenance and development of the individual, the society, or both. These are good reasons for participating in this kind of leisure, which leisure educators can pass on to the people they serve.

This is a good point to raise the question of whether leisure educators should also teach about the costs, and not just the rewards, associated with becoming involved in some way with a leisure organization. The answer is that they should, but not in the amount of detail needed to identify and discuss motivational rewards. A main premise of this book has been that, once people have a certain amount of favorable experience with a leisure activity, they find ways of defining its costs as less significant than its rewards. General acknowledgment by educators that some costs will emerge and will have to be dealt with should suffice. Since strong motivation to participate will often override them, it seems better to accent the positive as the best strategy for moving people toward an optimal leisure lifestyle. Consequently, it makes little sense to review here, in the same detail as has been done with the rewards, the various costs associated with organized leisure. Participants will discover them soon enough, and when they do, many will have developed the necessary positive outlook with which to counterbalance them.

Tribes

Do tribes, conceived of as a form of leisure organization, have import for leisure education? Surprisingly as it may seem, the answer is that they do.

Tribes are defined as fragmented groupings left over from the preceding era of mass consumption—groupings recognized today by their unique tastes and lifestyles. The raison d'être of the taste-based tribe is basically hedonic: it organizes a type of casual leisure that attracts and holds tribe members primarily through sociable conversation, sensory stimulation, or passive or active entertainment. Moreover, the question was raised in Chapter 5 as to whether the concept of tribe can be extended to such interest-based collectivities as hobbyists and sports enthusiasts. Can an activity, as opposed to a cultural taste, become the basis for a distinct tribe? We answered this question by determining where given collectivities fall on the continuum of structural complexity of organizations, which runs from the most elementary tribes at the pole of simplest organization to the most evolved social worlds at the opposite pole of most complex organization.

At its simplest a tribe is little more than an awareness among a mass of individuals that, in at least some other parts of the world, there are people who share the same special taste in music, clothing, bodily adornments, and similar items of mass culture. For this reason they feel a special attachment and belonging whenever any of them meet face to face. Adding newsletters, web sites, and so on increases the complexity of a tribe's organizational structure, which pushes it toward the social-world pole of the organization continuum.

Because serious leisure participants generally pursue their activities in highly complex organizational settings, the social world perspective was used to effect the most extensive and fruitful exploration possible (see Chapter 6). Since they are anything but scions of former mass consumption groupings, examining them within the tribal framework would have profoundly underestimated the complex motivational component found in the social world in which each activity is embedded. Still, all continua dealing with discrete, or separable, phenomena (as opposed to continuous phenomena like color or temperature) evoke the problem of the cutting point: where does one type end and another begin? Put differently, it was argued earlier that some serious leisure activities possibly fall closer to the tribal pole than others. The serious leisure activities found closest to the tribal pole are the various liberal arts hobbies (e.g., Trekkies, jazz buffs).

Should leisure educators therefore recommend that henceforth, to experience the unique rewards of this type of leisure organization, their clients and students rush out and attend a few raves? Not really. On the one hand, those interested in raves and similar tribes have no doubt already discovered them. No need here for leisure education on the matter. On the other hand, some people might nevertheless be unaware of tribes like the Trekkies and the devoted fans of soap opera, not to mention the buffs of certain sports, cuisines, and the fine and entertainment arts. This is casual leisure and, for some people, a good way to help fashion an optimal leisure lifestyle.

Social World

Unruh's (1979, 1980) idea of social world was defined in Chapter 1 as an entity composed of characteristic groups, events, routines, practices, and organizations. Each is held together, to an important degree, by semiformal or mediated communication. In other words, in the typical case, social worlds are neither heavily bureaucratized nor substantially organized through intense face-to-face interaction. Rather, communication commonly takes place indirectly by way of newsletters, posted notices, telephone messages, mass mailings, radio and television announcements, and similar means.

Yet, for some participants in these activities, the allied social world seems more like a kind of tribe than one of the complex entities that develops toward the other end of the continuum of organizational structure. That is, these participants know that other people share their leisure passion, that some of these people live in the same community and that many more live outside it in the same country or, in more and more these days, abroad. They also know that these kindred spirits share many of the same leisure habits and values.

Additionally, it was observed in Chapter 6 that, in themselves, serious leisure social worlds, when recognized as such, become highly attractive formations (Stebbins, 1999, p. 267), although they appear to inspire people more to stay in them than to join them in the first place. Because the idea is abstract, it usually takes a certain amount of time to learn about the social world of a complex leisure activity, something that, in fact, can only effectively occur once inside that world.

Indeed, nearly every serious leisure activity is anchored in a vibrant social world endowed with the capacity—once recognized—to attract and hold a large proportion of its participants. Although the activity itself is exciting, the excitement it generates is also greatly enhanced by the presence of networks of like-minded regulars and insiders, important strangers, local and national organizations, and emotionally charged spaces for pursuing the activity. Furthermore, various tourists visit from time to time—the audiences, spectators, admirers, onlookers, and others. Magazines, newsletters, courses, lectures, workshops, and similar channels of information make up another prominent part of the typical social world in serious leisure. It is important to disseminate these ideas about the motivational properties of leisure social worlds through the usual channels of leisure education.

Social Movements

Social movements were defined in Chapter 7 as noninstitutionalized sets of networks, small groups, and organizations that have coalesced around a significant value, which inspire members to promote or resist change with reference to it. Some, though by no means all, movements are primarily expressions of leisure involvement. As already mentioned, participation driven by strongly held negative emotions such as fear, hate, disgust, and revenge has the effect of overriding the definition of leisure as uncoerced activity, turning this so-called free time involvement into forced action. For social movement participation to be of the leisure variety, it must be undertaken because members positively want to do it, not because they negatively feel they have to do it, or they feel pressured. The emotions evoked should be on the order of love, joy, happiness, and the like. These are the entities that leisure educators will want to concern themselves with when discussing with the people they serve possible organizational opportunities for leisure participation.

Participation as leisure is amply evident in movements with goals like self or community development, realization of aesthetic values, or creation of a better life. As noted earlier, these movements, when truly leisure, are additive. In other words, they do not reach their goals eliminating something, as exemplified in the subtractive antismoking movement. Part of the job of leisure educator is to become familiar with a number of current social movements that might appeal to the people they serve as leisure outlets to which they could have relatively easy access.

Optimal Leisure Lifestyle

As mentioned in Chapter 1, a highly satisfying life of leisure is predicated, in part, on a workable schedule of all leisure activities as well as involvement in leisure organizations having substantial appeal. Optimally organized involvements will be temporally and geographically spaced in a way that participants avoid feeling harried while getting from one to another. Moreover, activities will be complementary, which often calls for variety. For instance, people fatigue after a sequence of too many physically or mentally demanding activities. For an optimal free-time existence, it is better to intersperse serious and casual leisure. Finally, the mix of activities changes over each person's life course, varying with such factors as age, sex, health, occupational demand, socioeconomic status, and place of residence.

Leisure education plays a prominent here as well. For without some kind of instruction or information on the nature and types of casual and serious leisure, most people are unlikely to acquire the information they need to choose the complement of activities that would compose their optimal leisure lifestyle. Such instruction or reading brings contact with the foregoing ideas about how leisure organizations can enhance this part of life. Fortunately, noncredit courses in this area are becoming ever more common. Many are being offered these days as lifestyle courses in adult education programs, while a book (Stebbins, 1998a) now provides detailed information on this way of taking leisure. Nonetheless, emphasis here is always on the individual and personal agency, giving people the opportunity to shape and reshape optimal leisure lifestyle; to draw on available social, educational, and monetary resources; and in serious leisure, to find a leisure career and participate in a social world.

Are We Bowling Alone?

Putnam (2000) has observed in the United States a declining number of members in voluntary organizations that require frequent, direct interaction with strangers, or nonmembers who members know little or not at all. He says, however, that the opposite trend holds for voluntary mass membership organizations, sometimes referred to as "tertiary organizations," which are well exemplified by the Sierra Club and the American Association of Retired Persons. Here, by contrast, for all but a few members, contact with strangers is never a problem.

Putnam argues that, more and more, it is like Americans are bowling alone, a sport normally played with at least one other person albeit now, figuratively speaking, one bereft of significant collective participation.

Being in a mass membership organization changes this indictment little since the typical individual member is essentially alone there. This person is content to pay dues and read disseminated information about the organization, while attending meetings of the group or becoming active in it as officer or committee member, for example, are not seen as pleasant ways to pass free time.

Putnam concluded that, on the organizational plane, Americans are becoming hermits of sorts [my term, not Putnam's], and that this tendency has serious consequences for civil society. We can say that a *civil society* is formed when a judicious balance between personal and communal interests exists in such a way that both individual liberty and social institutions are reasonably preserved. Principal among the consequences foreseen by Putnam is the fact that the social health of contemporary societies requires some strangers to interact some of time with each other. How else are their members going to obtain a direct understanding of who these people are and what they stand for socially, politically, religiously, and so forth? Are Americans, and for that matter citizens of other complex societies, really bowling alone these days as claimed? Are they really avoiding face-to-face contact with their compatriots beyond their own circles of family and friends?

Several studies contradict the Putnam argument, including an extensive fifteen-nation study by Baer, Curtis, and Grabb (2001). This book also argues that the answer to this question is, in fact, no. It does so by stressing that the concept of organization is far broader than the one examined by Putnam. Consider again Rocher's definition of organization from Chapter 1: the total arrangement of all the elements which serve to structure social action into a whole, which has an image or a particular form which is different from its constituent parts and also different from other possible arrangements. It was also observed that in leisure, as in many other areas of life, action is structured, or organized, in groups, social networks, and grassroots organizations as well as in larger complex organizations and still more broadly, in tribes, social worlds, and social movements. In short, the entire organizational spectrum properly considered, participation— bowling *with* others—appears to be most substantial. This notwithstanding evidence supplied by Putnam himself showing that participation in self-help groups and social movements has in fact grown, although not enough to offset the trend toward bowling alone (Putnam, 2000, pp. 148– 166, 180). Unfortunately, Putnam's analysis is limited, primarily because he relies on sets of survey data describing membership in formal entities only, thereby excluding from inquiry the multitude of informal dyads, triads, and small groups as well as tribes and social worlds on which no such data exist.

The main point to be made, then, in these the final pages of this book is the following. With respect to building and maintaining a civil society, participating in a leisure organization (as defined here) can also benefit in significant ways collective life and not, as argued to this point, just the individual participant. That is, by participating in this way, people engage in *civil labor:* "Voluntarily chosen socially necessary labor, designed to sustain the commons and reaffirm the individual's responsibilities and obligations to society" (Rojek, 2001, p. 122). However to deepen our understanding of this main point, we must consider two personal strategies for pursuing leisure in everyday life—selfishness and solitude.

Selfishness and Solitude

The first strategy is, whenever the need arises, to selfishly pursue leisure, both casual and serious. When someone defines an act as selfish, that person makes an imputation. This imputation is most commonly hurled at perceived self-seekers by their victims, where the self-seekers are felt to demonstrate a concern for their own welfare or advantage at the expense of or in disregard for their victims (Stebbins, 2001a, p. 81). The central thread running through the fabric of selfishness is exploitative unfairness—a kind of personal favoritism infecting our everyday affairs. Yet, as annoying as a selfish act can be, it is probably most accurately classified as a breach of etiquette (Cooley, 1922, p. 216) rather than as an instance of deviance, which is a significantly weightier moral transgression. Furthermore, a selfish act is goal-directed. Self-seekers have particular ends in mind, pursuit of which results in what others define as unfair exploitation.

When people selfishly pursue their leisure, they exploit others, some of whom may be in the same leisure organization. Friends and relatives have certainly been known to take unfair advantage of one another, just as individuals have been known to misuse a group in this way, be it small, grassroots, volunteer, or leisure service. According to this expanded definition of organization, such behavior can be said to undermine the building and maintenance of civil society on various levels of organizational complexity.

Bear in mind, however, that it is certainly possible to exploit others who are not in the same leisure organization and not the organization itself, as when a husband risks family money earmarked for the rent to gamble with his cronies at the Friday night poker session. This selfish act exploits the man's family, while weakening in its own small way the civil society in which it is embedded. Still, it does no damage to the cohesiveness of the poker group. Selfishness is probably always inimical in some way for civil society, but only inimical from time to time for leisure organization.

The second personal strategy—the pursuit of solitude—exists in a more complicated relationship with both civil society and leisure organization. It is the purest instance of bowling alone, in that it is both intentionally sought and hopefully facilitative (Stebbins, 1993b). Being free from the necessity of associating with others and from their distracting and inter-rupting activities, the individual is able to pursue most effectively personal interests or concerns. Loneliness, by contrast, is unwanted—no one seeks it. Privacy, of course, is wanted, but is distinguished by its protectiveness or secretiveness. There is something to hide, which is not typically a goal of aloneness, or solitude.

People want to be alone for one or more of three reasons: to accomplish a task or reach a goal; relax while away from people; or think about past, present, or future problems involving self or others. The first facilitates many forms of serious leisure (e.g., practicing a musical instrument, studying a textbook for an adult education course), whereas the second facilitates casual leisure achieved while, for instance, sitting, walking, or driving alone. The third reason could facilitate serious leisure, as in thinking alone about ways to find enough volunteers to run the annual church picnic or about effective strategies to win a basketball tournament. Just as likely, the third reason could facilitate reflection on a problem having little or nothing to do with leisure (e.g., how to tell your spouse you want a divorce, how to handle an overbearing employer).

Kandy James (2001) found that her sample of adolescent girls in west-ern Australia used their bedrooms to be alone for these purposes. This is where they can be themselves without an audience (e.g., to dance, sing, play guitar), and where they can hang out free of worry over their body image. This is where they can relax, think, and exercise without interruption. All this is possible because their bedrooms are spaces they control.

By definition, people in a state of solitude are not participating in orga-nized leisure or civil society. Yet, it would be naïve in many instances to say that this strategy harms either one. In fact, the orchestra will benefit from the aloneness found by its violinists to practice their parts. Likewise, relaxation is widely regarded as important for regenerating people for further work, after having already put in several hours on the job. If these sessions of practice and relaxation are enjoyed alone and are effective for that reason, so much the better.

In short, people seeking solitude are not loners, as this term is usually defined. Being alone is strategically sought as a temporary condition that, in manifold ways, eventually aids leisure organization and strengthens civil society. That is, provided it is not selfishly sought or used to reach selfish goals or hatch selfish strategies.

All this is evidence that motivation to participate in leisure organizations, whatever their size, has a personal side that we dare not neglect. These collectivities are powerfully attractive to many people, but some of these same people also react idiosyncratically to the strength of their magnetism. Acting selfishly and seeking aloneness are two ways that they do this. As we come to know more about the motivational properties of leisure organizations, we will likely discover more ways that people as individuals relate to them.

References

Aberle, D.F. (1966). *The peyote religion among the Navaho*. Chicago, IL: Aldine.

Aitchison, C. (2000). Young disabled people, leisure and everyday life: Reviewing conventional definitions for leisure studies. *Annals of Leisure Research, 3*, 1–20.

Amis, J., Slack, T., and Berrett, T. (1995). The structural antecedents of conflict in voluntary sport organizations. *Leisure Studies, 14*, 1–16.

Anderssen, N. and Wold, B. (1992). Parental and peer influences on leisure-time physical activity in young adolescents. *Research Quarterly for Exercise and Sport, 63*(4), 314–348.

Apostle, R. (1992). Curling for cash: The "professionalization" of a popular Canadian sport. *Culture, 12*(2), 17–28.

Arai, S.M. (1997). Volunteers within a changing society: The uses of empowerment theory in understanding serious leisure. *World Leisure and Recreation, 39*(3), 19–22.

Babrow, A.S. (1990). Audience motivation, viewing context, media content, and form: The interactional emergence of soap opera entertainment. *Communication Studies, 41*, 343–361.

Back, K.W. (1981). Small groups. In M. Rosenberg and R.H. Turner (Eds.), *Social psychology* (pp. 320–343). New York, NY: Basic Books.

Back to Godhead (1982). *17*(1), 30–31.

Baer, D., Curtis, J., and Grabb, E. (2001). Has voluntary association activity declined? Cross-national analyses for fifteen countries. *Canadian Review of Sociology and Anthropology, 38*, 275–292.

Baldwin, C.K. and Norris, P.A. (1999). Exploring the dimensions of serious leisure: "Love me—love my dog." *Journal of Leisure Research, 31*, 1–17.

Baldwin, J.H., Ellis, G.D., and Baldwin, B.M. (1999). Marital satisfaction: An examination of its relationship to spouse support and congruence of commitment among runners. *Leisure Sciences, 21*, 117–132.

Barnes, J.A. (1954). Class and committees in a Norwegian island parish. *Human Relations, 7*, 39–58.

Beaford, R.D., Gongaware, T.B., and Valadez, D.L. (2000). Social movements. In E.F. Borgatta and R.J.V. Mongomery (Eds.), *Encyclopedia of sociology, Vol. 4* (2nd ed., pp. 2717–2727). New York, NY: Macmillan Reference USA.

Bella, L. (1992). *The Christmas imperative: Leisure, family, and women's work.* Halifax, NS: Fernwood.

Bialeschki, M.D. and Pearce, K.D. (1997). I don't want a lifestyle—I want a life: The effect of role negotiations on the leisure of lesbian mothers. *Journal of Leisure Research, 29,* 113–131.

Bishop, J. and Hoggett, P. (1986). *Organizing around enthusiasms: Patterns of mutual aid in leisure.* London, UK: Comedia Publishing Group.

Blackshaw, T. and Long, J. (1998). A critical examination of the advantages of investigating community and leisure from a social network perspective. *Leisure Studies, 17,* 233–248.

Borgatta, E.F. (1981). The small groups movement. *American Behavioral Scientist, 24,* 265–271.

Bott, E. (1957). *Family and social network.* London, UK: Tavistock Publications.

Brattain Rogers, N. (1999). Family obligation, caregiving, and loss of leisure: The experiences of three caregivers. *Activities, Adaptation & Aging, 24*(2), 35.

Brown, M.E. (1994). *Soap opera and women's talk: The pleasure of resistance.* Thousand Oaks, CA: Sage Publications.

Butsch, R. (1984). The commodification of leisure: The case of the model airplane hobby and industry. *Qualitative Sociology, 7,* 217–235.

Caldwell, L.L., Kivel, B.D., Smith, E.A., and Hayes, D. (1998). The leisure context of adolescents who are lesbian, gay male, bisexual and questioning their sexual identities: An exploratory study. *Journal of Leisure Research, 30,* 341–355.

Clark, A. (1997, September 20). Comedy college. *Financial Post,* p. 36.

Cole, L.M. (1959). One astronomer's wife. *Sky & Telescope, 18*(1959), 137.

Cooley, C.H. (1922). *Human nature and the social order* (Rev. ed.). New York, NY: Charles Scribner's Sons.

Critcher, C. (2000). "Still raving:" Social reaction to ecstasy. *Leisure Studies, 19,* 145–162.

Cutler, S.J. and Danigelis, N.L. (1993). Organized contexts of activity. In J.R. Kelly (Ed.), *Activity and aging: Staying involved in later life* (pp. 146–163). Thousand Oaks, CA: Sage Publications.

Deegan, M.-J. (1983). A feminist frame analysis of "Star Trek." *Free Inquiry in Creative Sociology, 11,* 182–188.

Donnelly, P. (1994). Take my word for it: Trust in the context of birding and mountaineering. *Qualitative Sociology, 17,* 215–241.

Duke, C. (1994). Adult and continuing education. In T. Husén and T.N. Postlethwaite (Eds.), *The international encyclopedia of education: Vol. 1* (2nd ed., pp. 89–94). Tarrytown, NY: Elsevier Science.

Feinbloom, D.H. (1976). *Transvestites and transsexuals.* New York, NY: Delacourte Press/Seymour Lawrence.

Fine, G.A. (1979). Small groups and culture creation: The idioculture of Little League Baseball teams. *American Sociological Review, 44,* 733–745.

Fine, G.A. (1983). *Shared fantasy: Role-playing games as social worlds.* Chicago, IL: University of Chicago Press.

Fine, G.A. (1988). Dying for a laugh. *Western Folklore, 47,* 77–194.

Fine, G.A. (1989). Mobilizing fun: Provisioning resources in leisure worlds. *Sociology of Sport Journal, 6,* 319–334.

Fine, G.A. (1998). *Morel tales: The culture of mushrooming.* Cambridge, MA: Harvard University Press.

Fine, G.A. and Holyfield, L. (1996). Trusting fellows: Secrecy, trust, and voluntary allegiance in leisure spheres. *Social Psychological Quarterly, 59,* 22–38.

Finnegan, R. (1989). *The hidden musicians: Music-making in an English town.* Cambridge, UK: Cambridge University Press.

Flora, J. and Segrin, C. (1998). Joint leisure time in friend and romantic relationships: The role of activity type, social skills, and positivity. *Journal of Social and Personal Relationships, 15,* 711–718.

Floro, G.K. (1978). What to look for in a study of the volunteer in the work world. In R.P. Wolensky and E.J. Miller (Eds.), *The small city and regional community* (pp. 194–202). Stevens Point, WI: Foundation Press.

Friesen, B.K. (1990). Powerlessness in adolescence: Exploiting heavy metal listeners. In C.R. Sanders (Ed.), *Marginal conventions: Popular culture, mass media, and social deviance* (pp. 65–77). Bowling Green, OH: Bowling Green State University Popular Press.

Garbard, D.L. (1997). Volunteer burnout and dropout: Issues in AIDS service organizations. *Journal of Health and Human Services Administration, 19,* 283–303.

Glogow, E. (1986, Spring). Research note: Burnout and loss of control. *Public Personnel Management, 15,* 79–83.

Godbey, G. (1999). *Leisure in your life: An exploration* (5th ed.). State College, PA: Venture Publishing, Inc.

Goff, S.J., Fick, D.S., and Oppliger, R.A. (1997). The moderating effect of spouse support on the relation between serious leisure and spouses' perceived leisure-family conflict. *Journal of Leisure Research, 29,* 47–60.

Goffman, E. (1961). *Asylums: Essays on the social situation of mental patients and other inmates.* Garden City, NY: Doubleday.

Goffman, E. (1963). *Stigma: Notes on the management of spoiled identity.* Englewood Cliffs, NJ: Prentice Hall.

Green, E. (1998). Women doing friendship: An analysis of women's leisure as a site of identity construction, empowerment and resistance. *Leisure Studies, 17,* 171–186.

Hamilton-Smith, E. (1993). In the Australian bush: Some reflections on serious leisure. *World Leisure & Recreation, 35*(1), 10–13.

Harrington, M., Cuskelly, G., and Auld, C. (2000). Career volunteering in commodity-intensive serious leisure: Motorsport events and their dependence on volunteers/amateurs. *Loisir et Société/Society and Leisure, 23,* 421–452.

Harris, M. (1998). Doing it their way: Organizational challenges for voluntary associations. *Nonprofit and Voluntary Sector Quarterly, 27,* 144–158.

Hibbler, D.K. and Shinew, K.J. (2002). Interracial couples' experience of leisure: A social network approach. *Journal of Leisure Research, 34,* 135–156.

Hoggett, P. and Bishop, J. (1985). Leisure beyond the individual consumer. *Leisure Studies, 4,* 21–38.

Horna, J. (1994). *The study of leisure: An introduction.* Toronto, ON: Oxford University Press.

Hultsman, W.Z. (1993). Influence of others as barrier to recreation participation among early adolescents. *Journal of Leisure Research, 25,* 150–164.

James, K. (2001). "I just gotta have my own space!" The bedroom as a leisure site for adolescent girls. *Journal of Leisure Research, 33,* 71–90.

Jankowski, M.S. (1999). Getting into gangs. In E. Rubington and M.S. Weinberg (Eds.), *Deviance: The interactionist perspective* (7th ed., pp. 273–286). Needham Heights, MA: Allyn & Bacon.

Jarvis, N. and King, L. (1997). Volunteers in uniformed youth organizations. *World Leisure and Recreation,* 39(3), 6–10.

Katz, A.H. and Bender, E.I. (1990). *Helping one another: Self-help groups in a changing world.* Oakland, CA: Third Party Publishing.

Katz, J. (1998). *Seductions of crime: Moral and sensual attractions of doing evil.* New York, NY: Basic Books.

Kelly, J.R. (1983). *Leisure identities and interactions.* London, UK: George Allen & Unwin.

Kelly, J.R. and Godbey. G. (1992). *The sociology of leisure.* State College, PA: Venture Publishing, Inc.

King, F.L. (1997). *Why contemporary Texas women quilt: A link to the sociology of leisure.* Unpublished doctoral dissertation, University of Texas, Arlington.

Kleiber, D.A. (1999). *Leisure experience and human development: A dialectical interpretation.* New York, NY: Basic Books.

Kleiber, D.A. (2000). The neglect of relaxation. *Journal of Leisure Research, 32,* 82–86.

Kleiber, D.A., Caldwell, L.L., and Shaw, S.M. (1993). Leisure meanings in adolescence. *Loisir et Société/Society and Leisure, 16,* 99–114.

Kleidman, R. (1994). Volunteer activism and professionalism in social movement organizations. *Social Problems, 41,* 257–276.

Klein, A.M. (1986). Pumping iron: Crisis and contradiction in bodybuilding. *Sociology of Sport Journal, 3,* 112–133.

Lambert, R.D. (1995). Looking for genealogical motivation. *Families, 34*(2), 149–160.

Lambert, R.D. (1996). Doing family history. *Families, 35*(1), 11–25.

Larson, R.W., Gillman, S.A., and Richards, M.H. (1997). Divergent experiences of family leisure: Fathers, mothers, and young adolescents. *Journal of Leisure Research, 29,* 78–97.

Lengkeek, J. and Bargeman, B. (1997). Voluntary associations and leisure: At the core of social change. *Loisir et Société/Society and Leisure, 20,* 237–255.

Lepage, L. (2001). Le saint-laurent, théâtre d'une expérimentation. *Découvrir: La revue de la recherche, 22*(2), 34–37.

Lieberman, M.A., and Borman, L.D. with Bond, G.R., Antze, P., and Levy, L.H. (1979). *Self-help groups for coping with crises.* San Francisco, CA: Jossey-Bass.

Maffesoli, M. (1996). *The time of the tribes: The decline of individualism* (D. Smith, Trans.). London, UK: Sage Publications.

Maines, D.R. (1982). In search of mesostructure. *Urban Life, 11,* 267–279.

Mannell, R.C and Kleiber, D.A. (1997). *A social psychology of leisure.* State College, PA: Venture Publishing, Inc.

McCall, G.J. and Simmons, J.L. (1978). *Identities and interactions* (Rev. ed.). New York, NY: Free Press.

McCarthy, J.D. and Zald, M.N. (1987). Appendix: The trend of social movements in America: Professionalization and resource mobilization. In M.N. Zald and J.D. McCarthy (Eds.), *Social movements in organizational society: Collected essays* (pp. 337–392). New Brunswick, NJ: Transaction.

McKim, J.B. (1997, June 29). Keeping the revolution alive. *Boston Globe,* B2.

Melton, J.G. (1986). *Encyclopedic handbook of cults in America.* New York, NY: Garland.

Melton, J.G. (1992). *The encyclopedia of American religions.* Wilmington, DE: McGrath Publishing, Co.

Mitchell, R.G., Jr. (1983). *Mountain experience: The psychology and sociology of adventure.* Chicago. IL: University of Chicago Press.

Mittelstaedt, R.D. (1990/91). The Civil War reenactment: A growing trend in creative leisure behavior. *Leisure Information Quarterly, 17*(4), 4–6.

Mittelstaedt, R.D. (1995). Reenacting the American Civil War: A unique form of serious leisure for adults. *World Leisure and Recreation, 37*(1), 23–27.

Moreno, I. (2000). Creative leisure: A path for human development. In M.C. Cabeza (Ed.), *Leisure and human development: Proposals for the 6th World Leisure Congress* (pp. 85–90). Bilbao, Spain: University of Deusto.

Nahrstedt, W. (2000). Global edutainment: The role of leisure education for community development. In A. Sivan and H. Ruskin (Eds.), *Leisure education, community development and populations with special needs* (pp. 65–74). London, UK: CAB International.

Olmsted, A.D. (1988). Morally controversial leisure: The social world of gun collectors. *Symbolic Interaction, 11*, 277–288.

Olmsted, A.D. (1993, Spring). Hobbies and serious leisure. *World Leisure and Recreation, 35*, 27–32.

Orthner, D.K. (1975). Leisure activity patterns and marital satisfaction over the marital career. *Journal of Marriage and the Family, 37*, 91–104.

Pearce, J.L. (1993). *Volunteers: The organizational behavior of unpaid workers*. London, UK: Routledge.

Pinard, M. and Hamilton, R. (1986). In K. Lang and G.E. Lang (Eds.), *Research in social movements, conflicts, and change* (Vol. 9, pp. 225–280). Greenwich, CT: JAI.

Putnam, R.D. (2000). *Bowling alone: The collapse and revival of American community*. New York, NY: Simon & Schuster.

Ragheb, M.G. and Merydith, S.P. (2001). Development and validation of a multidimensional scale measuring free time boredom. *Leisure Studies, 20*, 41–60.

Rapoport, R. and Rapoport, R.N. (1978). *Leisure and the family life cycle*. London, UK: Routledge and Kegan Paul.

Roberts, K. (1997). Same activities, different meanings: British youth cultures in the 1990s. *Leisure Studies, 16*, 1–16.

Roberts, K. (1999). *Leisure in contemporary society*. New York, NY: CABI Publishing.

Rocher, G. (1972). *A general introduction to sociology: A theoretical perspective* (P. Sheriff, Trans.). Toronto, ON: Macmillan Canada.

Rojek, C. (2001). Leisure and life politics. *Leisure Sciences, 23*, 115–126.

Romeder, J.-M. (1990). *The self-help way: Mutual aid and health*. Ottawa, ON: Canadian Council on Social Development.

Scott, D. and Godbey, G.C. (1992). An analysis of adult play groups: Social versus serious participation in contract bridge. *Leisure Sciences, 14*, 47–67.

Selman, G., Cooke, M., Selman, M., and Dampier, P. (1998). *The foundations of adult education in Canada* (2nd ed.). Toronto, ON: Thompson Educational Publishing.

Shaw, S.M. (2001). Conceptualizing resistance: Women's leisure as political practice. *Journal of Leisure Research, 33,* 186–201.

Shaw, S.M., Caldwell, L.L., and Kleiber, D.A. (1996). Boredom, stress and social control in the daily activities of adolescents. *Journal of Leisure Research, 28,* 274–292.

Shields, R. (1996). Foreword. In M. Maffesoli, *The time of the tribes: The decline of individualism* (D. Smith, Trans.). London, UK: Sage Publications.

Smith, D.H. (1994). Determinants of voluntary association participation and volunteering: A literature review. *Nonprofit and Voluntary Sector Quarterly, 23,* 243–264.

Smith, D.H. (1997). The rest of the nonprofit sector: Grassroots associations as the dark matter ignored in prevailing "flat earth" maps of the sector. *Nonprofit and Voluntary Sector Quarterly, 26,* 114–131.

Smith, D.H. (2000). *Grassroots associations.* Thousand Oaks, CA: Sage Publications.

Smith, D.H. (in press). *Organizations on the fringe: Understanding deviant nonprofits as part of a round-earth paradigm of the voluntary nonprofit sector.* Thousand Oaks, CA: Sage Publications.

Snow, D.A. and Malachek, R. (1984). The sociology of conversion. In R.H. Turner and J.F. Short, Jr., *Annual review of sociology* (Vol. 10, pp. 167–190). Palo Alto, CA: Annual Reviews Inc.

Snyder, E.E. (1986). The social world of shuffleboard. *Urban Life, 15,* 237–253.

Stebbins, R.A. (1976). Music among friends: The social networks of amateur musicians. *International Review of Sociology (Series II), 12,* 52–73.

Stebbins, R.A. (1979). *Amateurs: On the margin between work and leisure.* Thousand Oaks, CA: Sage Publications.

Stebbins, R.A. (1980). Avocational science: The amateur routine in archaeology and astronomy. *International Journal of Comparative Sociology, 21,* 34–48.

Stebbins, R.A. (1981). Toward a social psychology of stage fright. In M. Hart and S. Birrell (Eds.), *Sport in the sociocultural process* (pp. 156–163). Dubuque, IA: W.C. Brown.

Stebbins, R.A. (1990). *The laugh-makers: Stand-up comedy as art, business, and lifestyle.* Montréal, PQ and Kingston, ON: McGill-Queen's University Press.

Stebbins, R.A. (1992). *Amateurs, professionals, and serious leisure.* Montréal, PQ and Kingston, ON: McGill-Queen's University Press.

Stebbins, R.A. (1993a). *Canadian football. A view from the helmet* (reprinted ed.). Toronto, ON: Canadian Scholars Press.

Stebbins, R.A. (1993b). *Predicaments: Moral difficulty in everyday life.* Lanham, MD: University Press of America.

Stebbins, RA. (1993c). *Career, culture and social psychology in a variety art: The magician.* Malabar, FL: Krieger.

Stebbins, RA. (1993d, Spring). Social world, life-style, and serious leisure: Toward a mesostructural analysis. *World Leisure and Recreation, 35,* 23–26.

Stebbins, R.A. (1994). The liberal arts hobbies: A neglected subtype of serious leisure. *Loisir et Société/Society and Leisure, 16,* 173–186.

Stebbins, R.A. (1996a). *The barbershop singer: Inside the social world of a musical hobby.* Toronto, ON: University of Toronto Press.

Stebbins, R.A. (1996b). *Tolerable differences: Living with deviance* (2nd ed.). Toronto, ON: McGraw-Hill Ryerson.

Stebbins, R.A. (1996c). Volunteering: A serious leisure perspective. *Nonprofit and Voluntary Action Quarterly, 25,* 211–224.

Stebbins, R.A. (1996d). Casual and serious leisure and post-traditional thought in the information age. *World Leisure and Recreation, 38*(3), 4–11.

Stebbins, R.A. (1997a). Casual leisure: A conceptual statement. *Leisure Studies, 16,* 17–25.

Stebbins, R.A. (1997b). Lifestyle as a generic concept in ethnographic research. *Quality and Quantity, 31,* 347–360.

Stebbins, R.A. (1998a). *After work: The search for an optimal leisure lifestyle.* Calgary, AB: Detselig Enterprises.

Stebbins, R.A. (1998b). *The urban francophone volunteer: Searching for personal meaning and community growth in a linguistic minority.* (New Scholars–New Visions in Canadian Studies quarterly monographs series, Vol. 3, No. 2). Seattle, WA: University of Washington, Canadian Studies Centre.

Stebbins, R.A. (1999, July–September). Encouraging youthful involvement in the arts: A serious leisure framework. *Lo Spettacolo, 49,* 261–275.

Stebbins, R.A. (2000a). Optimal leisure lifestyle: Combining serious and casual leisure for personal well-being. In M.C. Cabeza (Ed.), *Leisure and human development: Proposals for the 6th World Leisure Congress* (pp. 101–107). Bilbao, Spain: University of Deusto.

Stebbins, R.A. (2000b). Obligation as an aspect of leisure experience. *Journal of Leisure Research, 32*, 152–155.

Stebbins, R.A. (2000c). Introduction: Antinomies in volunteering—Choice/ obligation, leisure/work. *Loisir et Société/Society and Leisure, 23,* 313–324.

Stebbins, R.A. (2001a). New directions in the theory and research of serious leisure. *Mellen Studies in Sociology, 28.* Lewiston, NY: Edwin Mellen Press.

Stebbins, R.A. (2001b). *Exploratory research in the social sciences.* (Sage University Paper Series on Qualitative Research Methods, Vol. 48). Thousand Oaks, CA: Sage Publications.

Stebbins, R.A. (2001c). The costs and benefits of hedonism: Some consequences of taking casual leisure seriously. *Leisure Studies, 20,* 305–309.

Stokowski, P.A. (1994). *Leisure in society: A network structural perspective.* New York, NY: Mansell Publishing.

Stokowski, P.A. and Lee, R.G. (1991). The influence of social network ties on recreation and leisure: An exploratory study. *Journal of Leisure Research, 23,* 95–113.

Stoner, C. and Parke, J.A. (1977). *All God's children: The cult experience— Salvation or slavery?* Radnor, PA: Chilton.

Taylor, B. (1995). Amateurs, professionals, and the knowledge of archaeology. *British Journal of Sociology, 46,* 499–508.

The Family. (2001, May). The fundamental beliefs of The Family. Retrieved from http://www.thefamily.org/about/beliefs.php#top

Thompson, M.C. (1997). *Volunteer firefighters: Our silent heroes.* Unpublished doctoral dissertation, Department of Sociology, University of Calgary.

Turner, R.H. and Killian, L.M. (1987). *Collective behavior* (3rd ed.). Englewood Cliffs, NJ: Prentice Hall.

Unruh, D.R. (1979). Characteristics and types of participation in social worlds. *Symbolic Interaction, 2,* 115–130.

Unruh, D.R. (1980). The nature of social worlds. *Pacific Sociological Review, 23,* 271–296.

Van Til, J. (1988). *Mapping the third sector: Voluntarism in a changing political economy*. New York, NY: The Foundation Center.

Weber, T.R. (1999). Raving in Toronto: Peace, love, unity, and respect in transition. *Journal of Youth Studies, 2*, 317–336.

Wilson, K. (1995). Olympians or lemmings? The postmodernist fun run. *Leisure Studies, 14*, 174–185.

Woodhouse, A. (1989). *Fantastic women: Sex, gender, and transvestism*. New Brunswick, NJ: Rutgers University Press.

Yiannakis, A. and Gibson, H. (1992). Roles tourists play. *Annals of Tourism Research, 19*, 287–303.

Yoder, D.G. (1997). A model for commodity intensive serious leisure. *Journal of Leisure Research, 29*, 407–429.

Zurcher, L.A. and Snow, D.A. (1981). Collective behavior: Social movements. In M. Rosenberg and R.H. Turner (Eds.), *Social psychology* (pp. 447–482). New York, NY: Basic Books.

Appendix

The Professional-Amateur-Public (P-A-P) System

One main way of defining amateurs within the serious leisure perspective has been to view them as part of a professional-amateur-public (P-A-P) system of interdependent relationships—an institutional location that is both cause and effect of their serious, committed orientation toward the activity in question. In any particular art, science, sport, or field of entertainment, it is evident that amateurs are linked to professionals or their public or both in at least seven ways which, to avoid needless repetition, are only summarized here. (For more detail, see Stebbins, 1979, pp. 27–33; 1992, pp. 38–41.)

1. Amateurs serve a public, as professionals do, and at times the same one. Here they are guided by standards of excellence set and communicated by the professionals.

2. A monetary and organizational relationship exists between amateurs and professionals, as when professionals train, advise, organize, and even perform with amateurs, and when amateurs come to constitute a special, knowledgeable part of the professionals' public.

3. Intellectual ties bind these two groups, which spring primarily from the amateurs who can maintain a broader and simultaneously less specialized knowledge of the field than can most professionals. Professionals must concentrate on those activities that provide a living, which often consume all the time they care to devote to their work.

4. Amateurs restrain professionals from overemphasizing technique and from stressing superficialities in place of profound work or products.

5. Amateurs insist on the retention of excellence.

6. Amateurs often stimulate professionals to give the public the best they can.

7. Professionals who form part of a P-A-P system inevitably start in the amateur ranks, as pure amateurs or preprofessional

amateurs; unless they abandon their field altogether or die in it; they also return to those ranks at a later stage in their career.

Yoder's study (1997) of tournament bass fishing in the United States resulted in an extension of this definition. He showed, first, that fishers here are amateurs, not hobbyists, and second, that commodity producers serving both amateur and professional tournament fishers play a role significant enough to justify a modification in the original triangular P-A-P system of relationships. His more complicated triangular model consisted of a system of relationships between commodity agents, professionals/commodity agents, and amateurs/publics (C-PC-AP system). Nevertheless, as noted on pages 74–75 of this book, where the C-PC-AP model is more thoroughly discussed, the P-A-P model still fits best a large number of amateur-professional fields.

Index

The A•B•Cs of Behavior Change: Skills for Working With Behavior Problems in Nursing Homes
by Margaret D. Cohn, Michael A. Smyer, and Ann L. Horgas

Activity Experiences and Programming Within Long-Term Care
by Ted Tedrick and Elaine R. Green

The Activity Gourmet
by Peggy Powers

Advanced Concepts for Geriatric Nursing Assistants
by Carolyn A. McDonald

Adventure Programming
edited by John C. Miles and Simon Priest

Assessment: The Cornerstone of Activity Programs
by Ruth Perschbacher

Behavior Modification in Therapeutic Recreation: An Introductory Manual
by John Dattilo and William D. Murphy

Benefits of Leisure
edited by B. L. Driver, Perry J. Brown, and George L. Peterson

Benefits of Recreation Research Update
by Judy M. Sefton and W. Kerry Mummery

Beyond Bingo: Innovative Programs for the New Senior
by Sal Arrigo, Jr., Ann Lewis, and Hank Mattimore

Beyond Bingo 2: More Innovative Programs for the New Senior
by Sal Arrigo, Jr.

Both Gains and Gaps: Feminist Perspectives on Women's Leisure
by Karla Henderson, M. Deborah Bialeschki, Susan M. Shaw, and Valeria J. Freysinger

Client Assessment in Therapeutic Recreation Services
by Norma J. Stumbo

Conceptual Foundations for Therapeutic Recreation
edited by David R. Austin, John Dattilo, and Bryan P. McCormick

Dimensions of Choice: A Qualitative Approach to Recreation, Parks, and Leisure Research
by Karla A. Henderson

Diversity and the Recreation Profession: Organizational Perspectives
edited by Maria T. Allison and Ingrid E. Schneider

Effective Management in Therapeutic Recreation Service
by Gerald S. O'Morrow and Marcia Jean Carter

Everything From A to Y: The Zest Is up to You! Older Adult Activities for Every Day of the Year
by Nancy R. Cheshire and Martha L. Kenney

Evaluating Leisure Services: Making Enlightened Decisions, Second Edition
by Karla A. Henderson and M. Deborah Bialeschki

The Evolution of Leisure: Historical and Philosophical Perspectives
by Thomas Goodale and Geoffrey Godbey

Experience Marketing: Strategies for the New Millennium
by Ellen L. O'Sullivan and Kathy J. Spangler

Facilitation Techniques in Therapeutic Recreation
by John Dattilo

File o' Fun: A Recreation Planner for Games & Activities, Third Edition
by Jane Harris Ericson and Diane Ruth Albright

The Game and Play Leader's Handbook: Facilitating Fun and Positive Interaction
by Bill Michaelis and John M. O'Connell

The Game Finder—A Leader's Guide to Great Activities
by Annette C. Moore

Getting People Involved in Life and Activities: Effective Motivating Techniques
by Jeanne Adams

Glossary of Recreation Therapy and Occupational Therapy
by David R. Austin

Other Books by Venture Publishing, Inc.

Great Special Events and Activities
by Annie Morton, Angie Prosser, and
Sue Spangler

Group Games & Activity Leadership
by Kenneth J. Bulik

Growing with Care: Using Greenery, Gardens and Nature with Aging and Special Populations
by Betsy Kreidler

Hands on! Children's Activities for Fairs, Festivals, and Special Events
by Karen L. Ramey

Inclusive Leisure Services: Responding to the Rights of People with Disabilities, Second Edition
by John Dattilo

Innovations: A Recreation Therapy Approach to Restorative Programs
by Dawn R. De Vries and Julie M. Lake

Internships in Recreation and Leisure Services: A Practical Guide for Students, Third Edition
by Edward E. Seagle, Jr. and Ralph W. Smith

Interpretation of Cultural and Natural Resources
by Douglas M. Knudson, Ted T. Cable, and Larry Beck

Intervention Activities for At-Risk Youth
by Norma J. Stumbo

Introduction to Recreation and Leisure Services, 8th Edition
by Karla A. Henderson, M. Deborah Bialeschki, John L. Hemingway, Jan S. Hodges, Beth D. Kivel, and H. Douglas Sessoms

Introduction to Writing Goals and Objectives: A Manual for Recreation Therapy Students and Entry-Level Professionals
by Suzanne Melcher

Leadership and Administration of Outdoor Pursuits, Second Edition
by Phyllis Ford and James Blanchard

Leadership in Leisure Services: Making a Difference, Second Edition
by Debra J. Jordan

Leisure and Leisure Services in the 21st Century
by Geoffrey Godbey

The Leisure Diagnostic Battery: Users Manual and Sample Forms
by Peter A. Witt and Gary Ellis

Leisure Education I: A Manual of Activities and Resources, Second Edition
by Norma J. Stumbo

Leisure Education II: More Activities and Resources, Second Edition
by Norma J. Stumbo

Leisure Education III: More Goal-Oriented Activities
by Norma J. Stumbo

Leisure Education IV: Activities for Individuals with Substance Addictions
by Norma J. Stumbo

Leisure Education Program Planning: A Systematic Approach, Second Edition
by John Dattilo

Leisure Education Specific Programs
by John Dattilo

Leisure in Your Life: An Exploration, Fifth Edition
by Geoffrey Godbey

Leisure Services in Canada: An Introduction, Second Edition
by Mark S. Searle and Russell E. Brayley

Leisure Studies: Prospects for the Twenty-First Century
edited by Edgar L. Jackson and Thomas L. Burton

The Lifestory Re-Play Circle: A Manual of Activities and Techniques
by Rosilyn Wilder

Models of Change in Municipal Parks and Recreation: A Book of Innovative Case Studies
edited by Mark E. Havitz

More Than a Game: A New Focus on Senior Activity Services
by Brenda Corbett

Nature and the Human Spirit: Toward an Expanded Land Management Ethic
edited by B. L. Driver, Daniel Dustin, Tony Baltic, Gary Elsner, and George Peterson

Outdoor Recreation Management: Theory and Application, Third Edition
by Alan Jubenville and Ben Twight

Planning Parks for People, Second Edition
by John Hultsman, Richard L. Cottrell, and Wendy Z. Hultsman

The Process of Recreation Programming Theory and Technique, Third Edition
by Patricia Farrell and Herberta M. Lundegren

Programming for Parks, Recreation, and Leisure Services: A Servant Leadership Approach
by Donald G. DeGraaf, Debra J. Jordan, and Kathy H. DeGraaf

Protocols for Recreation Therapy Programs
edited by Jill Kelland, along with the Recreation Therapy Staff at Alberta Hospital Edmonton

Quality Management: Applications for Therapeutic Recreation
edited by Bob Riley

A Recovery Workbook: The Road Back from Substance Abuse
by April K. Neal and Michael J. Taleff

Recreation and Leisure: Issues in an Era of Change, Third Edition
edited by Thomas Goodale and Peter A. Witt

Recreation Economic Decisions: Comparing Benefits and Costs, Second Edition
by John B. Loomis and Richard G. Walsh

Recreation for Older Adults: Individual and Group Activities
by Judith A. Elliott and Jerold E. Elliott

Recreation Programming and Activities for Older Adults
by Jerold E. Elliott and Judith A. Sorg-Elliott

Reference Manual for Writing Rehabilitation Therapy Treatment Plans
by Penny Hogberg and Mary Johnson

Research in Therapeutic Recreation: Concepts and Methods
edited by Marjorie J. Malkin and Christine Z. Howe

Simple Expressions: Creative and Therapeutic Arts for the Elderly in Long-Term Care Facilities
by Vicki Parsons

A Social History of Leisure Since 1600
by Gary Cross

A Social Psychology of Leisure
by Roger C. Mannell and Douglas A. Kleiber

Steps to Successful Programming: A Student Handbook to Accompany Programming for Parks, Recreation, and Leisure Services
by Donald G. DeGraaf, Debra J. Jordan, and Kathy H. DeGraaf

Stretch Your Mind and Body: Tai Chi as an Adaptive Activity
by Duane A. Crider and William R. Klinger

Therapeutic Activity Intervention with the Elderly: Foundations & Practices
by Barbara A. Hawkins, Marti E. May, and Nancy Brattain Rogers

Therapeutic Recreation and the Nature of Disabilities
by Kenneth E. Mobily and Richard MacNeil

Therapeutic Recreation: Cases and Exercises, Second Edition
by Barbara C. Wilhite and M. Jean Keller

Therapeutic Recreation in Health Promotion and Rehabilitation
by John Shank and Catherine Coyle

Therapeutic Recreation in the Nursing Home
by Linda Buettner and Shelley L. Martin

Therapeutic Recreation Protocol for Treatment of Substance Addictions
by Rozanne W. Faulkner

Tourism and Society: A Guide to Problems and Issues
by Robert W. Wyllie

A Training Manual for Americans with Disabilities Act Compliance in Parks and Recreation Settings
by Carol Stensrud

 Venture Publishing, Inc.
1999 Cato Avenue
State College, PA 16801
phone: 814–234–4561
fax: 814–234–1651